# THE PILGRIMAGE OF FAITH
## of Tanzania Mennonite Church,
## 1934-83

# THE PILGRIMAGE OF FAITH
## of Tanzania Mennonite Church, 1934-83

Mahlon M. Hess

TANZANIA MENNONITE CHURCH
Musoma and Tarime, Tanzania

EASTERN MENNONITE BOARD
OF MISSIONS AND CHARITIES
Salunga, Pennsylvania 17538-0628

Scripture quotations, unless otherwise noted, are
from the Revised Standard Version of the Bible,
©1946, 1952, 1971, 1973

Library of Congress Catalog Card Number: 85-080354
International Standard Book Number 0-9613368-2-X
Printed in the United States of America

**DEDICATION:**

John E. Leatherman

Ezekiel K. and Raheri Muganda

Elam W. Stauffer

Phebe Yoder

Edna S. Hurst

Susana A. Kisare

# CONTENTS

# GLOSSARY

| | |
|---|---|
| AIM | Africa Inland Mission |
| AMBCF | Africa Mennonite and Brethren in Christ Fellowship |
| CCT | Christian Council of Tanganyika/Tanzania |
| CMS | Church Missionary Society |
| EMBMC | Eastern Mennonite Board of Missions and Charities |
| GC | General Conference Mennonite Church |
| KCMC | Kilimanjaro Christian Medical Center |
| LMC | Lancaster Mennonite Conference |
| LMEC | Lake Missions Education Council |
| MB | Mennonite Brethren |
| MBM | Mennonite Board of Missions |
| MCC | Mennonite Central Committee |
| SDA | Seventh-day Adventist |
| TANU | Tanganyika African National Union |
| TMC | Tanganyika/Tanzania Mennonite Church |
| TMCYL | TMC Youth League |
| UKWATA | Christian Union of Tanzania |

# INTRODUCTION

As God's people pass through life with its difficulties, sometimes they have to wonder how it all fits together. But many times when one looks back it is easy to trace the hand of the Lord, preparing and fulfilling his purposes. The fiftieth anniversary provides to Tanzania Mennonite Church (TMC) an excellent opportunity to look back and see what God has accomplished and to try to discern his purposes for the days ahead.

In 1974 David Shenk wrote *Mennonite Safari* to mark the fortieth anniversary of TMC—known in Swahili as Kanisa la Mennonite Tanzania (KMT). In the introduction I supported his hope that at an early date a Tanzanian would write the story as Tanzanians experienced it. I was surprised, then, to receive the request of Bishop Kisare and Bishop Sarya for me to prepare a book for the jubilee. This is indeed an honor which I accepted with some hesitancy, praying for grace to do justice to the project. I gave myself anew to the Lord, praying for his grace. I am happy to have had one more opportunity to serve Tanzania Mennonite Church, recognizing that recording the story will make it available to Mennonites around the world.

I thank God for three preparatory experiences. In a seminar a Tanzania colleague, Bishop Bengt Sundkler, who served with the Lutherans of Bukoba, cited a number of occasions when God first brought the gospel to a people through a national Christian, and soon after brought missionaries to share in the planting of the church.

In a study group in another setting, Donald Jacobs showed that while new churches come into being by particular initiatives of God, even the second generation needs to look again at how God worked and to accept these events as part of their own history.

In expressing his interest and support just before my Tanzania research, David Thomas urged, "We want to know this church—and keep the gospel in the story." That gave me a perspective—to understand history in the light of the gospel. So I watched for God's initiatives and tried to evaluate man's responses. I began to perceive the whole of human history as God dealing with man's disobediences, making obedience possible, and nudging man to respond in obedience. Against that backdrop I have placed the story of TMC. Using free verse I try to spell out that backdrop. At the end of chapter 1, I show how God overcame man's disobedience, with its implications for the nature of our pilgrimage, for church planting. At the beginning of chapter 10, I note the caravan of faith throughout the whole of world history. At the end of the chapter I speak to what it costs to participate in the pilgrimage, emphasizing that Jesus who leads the caravan will bring it to a consummation of blessedness.

To review the life of TMC in the light of the gospel calls for the experiences and reflections of many brothers and sisters, how they saw God at work among them. A mere recital of events and dates is inadequate; I was eager that together we see the hand of God and discern his purposes.

Though there were travel difficulties, God gave me opportunity to visit sixteen of the twenty church districts. Through youth choirs, testimonies, and interviews, we began to celebrate this jubilee. We meditated upon Ephesians 2, praising God for making us new persons, a part of his family. In Psalm 78 we noted the duty of parents and leaders to recount the mighty acts of God to children, grandchildren, and great-grandchildren. In a number of districts, I met with the church councils; in others, I perused minutes and other records. There were personal interviews with the pastors of the four small districts I could not visit. Through all the meetings I was greatly blessed.

Through our fellowship and discussions, there emerged four purposes for the book:

    a. To recall the experiences God has given and to praise him.
    b. To help church leaders assess what has been helpful and what might need to be strengthened or corrected.
    c. To tell the story to coming generations.
    d. To serve as a point of reference for future historians.

After a good start at the writing and some consultations with my Tanzanian advisers, it became necessary for me to return home. Then I had opportunity to review the mass of information made available to me and to read some of the letters circulated by the early missionaries and some of their reports to the mission board. I also spent some time refreshing myself in the Word of God and in church history, noting the overarching purposes of God. It was reassuring to sense how he is working out these same purposes in TMC.

A few explanations are in order:

a. In the span of TMC history I noted six events that stand out like mountaintops: the coming of the first missionaries, the beginnings of revival, the church unity in which the first pastors were discerned, the full autonomy of the church, its climax in the choice of the first national bishop, and the death of Muganda. So I have built my narrative around these major events, using each as the beginning of a new chapter.

b. I have attempted to give the picture of the total church. Many events are covered very briefly; for others there was no space.

c. While I usually name only one or two people in connection with an event or subject, they represent a host of others who were also involved. Further, I have mentioned persons whom God used for a time even though at present they are away from the Lord. May this book be a reminder to pray for those persons.

d. My TMC counselors reminded me that in human history some events are good and others are not praiseworthy; following the example of the Bible, I should record some of each. I was encouraged in this approach when in a police office I saw a poster highlighting one of the guidelines of the national political party: "To admit a weakness does not further weaken one; rather it shows self-confidence and readiness to correct one's self."

e. I recognize that, as one of the participants in the story, I cannot be objective in evaluating many of the events. Others will need to carry this role.

f. While this book reflects the experiences and viewpoints of many brothers and sisters, I am fully responsible for what has been selected and the way it is told. I beg forbearance for any shortcomings and mistakes, and stand ready to correct them.

I am indebted to many, many people. God abundantly answered my prayer that a goodly number of those who participated in the development of the church would contribute to the book. I hereby record my thanks to all who prepared papers on the subjects I suggested, those who contributed through interviews, and others whose writings were available to me. These persons are named in Appendix IV; I apologize to anyone who may have been overlooked. I am most grateful to the district pastors and council secretaries who prepared helpful reports. I thank the youth choirs for their efforts to tell parts of the story in original songs. I also thank each person who submitted photographs for my discretionary use.

I thank my advisory committees for overall guidance and for the numerous ways in which they helped: Bishop Kisare, Nashon Nyambok, Naftali Birai, Bishop Sarya, Daniel Mtoka, Eliasafu Igira, Nathanael Tingayi, Mutaragara Chirangi, Jairo Onyiego, Eliam Mauma, Hershey Leaman, David Shenk, Catharine Leatherman, John and Ruth Mosemann, Donald Jacobs, and Nathan Hege.

Since this book is in part a translation of the Swahili edition, and a rewrite of chapters 1, 2, and 10, I am indebted to all who contributed to the process. Anna Mae Kendig, Naomi Smoker, and Glen and Sylvia Hess assisted in research. Naomi Smoker, Jeanette Mummau, Jolita Ondura, Stella Newswanger, Linda Knouse, and Arlene Heistand did much of the typing. Manuscripts were checked by Emmanuel Muganda, Christopher Ndege, Yohana and Josiah Kawira, Clyde Shenk, Catharine Leatherman, Grace Stauffer, Joseph Shenk, Daniel Wenger, and other missionary colleagues, and also by Leonard Gross, Grace Wenger, and Paul Kraybill. Janet Gehman gave excellent editorial help. Mary Ebersole designed the cover and photo section; Naomi Weaver prepared the maps and graph. Larry Zook, David Fretz, and Harold Reed helped with logistics. I am grateful to Roy James and colleagues of York Graphic Services for their work on the photo section and statistical appendix, and to Stanley Yoder and colleagues of Mennonite Publishing House for printing and binding.

This records special appreciation to my congregation, Masonville Mennonite Church, and to my wife, Mabel, for releasing me for six months of field research, and for bearing with my unavailability during the months of writing, translating, and editing. Many shared with me as prayer helpers. May God richly bless all who had a part.

Let us continue to pray that this recital of the history of Tanzania Mennonite Church may glorify the Lord Jesus.

# 1.

# AWARENESS OF GOD

**Perception that disobedience separates man and God**

The Jita people of Tanzania, who live on the eastern shore of Lake Victoria, have a legend which says that in the beginning God was near to his people at all times. He manifested his presence by growing up as a young plant in any of the places designated for prayers and offerings. Such places could be approached only by priests chosen by God himself.

Whenever special difficulties came—lack of rain, sickness, attack by enemies—the whole community refrained from their usual work; they avoided aimless loitering and ate no food. The priests offered special prayers, naming the specific need.

After two days they would return to see whether God had heard their petitions. When they found that a glistening plant had sprung up in their place of worship, they believed that God had heard them and was showing himself ready to supply their need. They had experienced many times that when they prayed for rain, there came abundant rains; when they prayed about an epidemic, it came to an end. So the people believed that God was near and trusted him for what they needed.

One day a Jita woman experienced a problem she did not want others to know about. Early the next morning she went secretly to a place for worship among a grove of trees. With a troubled spirit she prayed and wept. There was no answer, and she went away in sorrow. On the following day she went earlier. In deep distress she threw herself down, pleading her difficulty, but again there was no response.

On the third day she went still earlier. This time she found a plant one foot high which had sprung up right in the center of the place of worship. Marveling greatly, she waited, expecting the solution for her problem. The plant held her attention because its color changed every minute.

Finally, weary of waiting for an answer, she reached out and touched the plant, but with great fear. Still there was no answer. Noting

15

the approach of dawn, and concerned not to be seen in the place reserved for priests, she boldly grabbed the plant and broke it off.

Immediately the whole land quaked, heavy claps of thunder reverberated, lightning flashed in the clouds, rocks rolled down the mountainsides, strong winds blew, streams overflowed. People were screaming, birds were screeching, and cattle were lowing.

After a time calm returned. The priests rushed to the place of worship to discover why God was angry. They were startled to find the woman, trembling with fear and holding in her hand the plant she had broken off.

The priests cried loudly, praying God not to place a curse on land or people because of the terrible offense of the woman. They gave orders that no one may work or leave his place, because God had been angered. Though they prayed and cried for a long time, nothing changed. God did not show his presence or answer their prayers as he had done so many times.

That was the last time God interacted with man. Since then, he has been far away, heard in earthquakes, in thunder and lightning and rain. They are his reminders that he has withdrawn from man because the means by which he had been coming and communicating had been abused![1]

Numerous tribes have a similar legend to explain why God now seems far away.

### Failure to follow the light

Even though the peoples of East Lake believe in a Creator God, they, like men everywhere, follow fleshly desires and tribal customs. In the past, tribal markings were very important: some stretched their ear lobes, others filed their teeth, others removed the lower six front teeth, and still others made markings on their face and/or body. Youth readily followed these customs so that they would be accepted in the tribe. They also participated in shameful deeds because everyone else did, and they wanted to associate with their peers. Everyone was brought up in these ways and had no idea of anything better.

In their preaching, African evangelists often reveal the exceeding darkness of sin. Zedekia Marwa Kisare, the first Tanzanian Mennonite bishop, has described life before the gospel came.

> All were liars and backbiters. Not one person trusted another. Rather they bewitched one another, sometimes out of fear and sometimes to settle

a conflict. They lived in fear of death, in fear of evil spirits. They worshiped ancestral spirits and demon powers, offering many sacrificial animals and much beer. In such deep darkness they hid themselves.

They were bound, not so much by taboos and tribal customs, but by Satan, his angels, and the ancestral spirits, who made the customs attractive. It is impossible to be released from such darkness and bondage except by a revelation of the mighty power of God.[2]

The offerings mentioned by Kisare were efforts for restoration of fellowship with God. But, like Old Testament offerings, they were powerless to remove guilt or change lives.

### God reaches out

In the midst of such darkness, individual Africans experienced God reaching out to them. Several East Lake persons have shared recollections from their past.

Bishop Kisare sometimes mentions questions which plagued him while growing up, Marwa the goat-herder, in his father's village at Kirongwe, North Mara: "Why am I here? Who am I? From where did I come?" In a late childhood reverie in the warmth of the early morning sun, there came the revelation: "There is a God; that is why I am here."

Yakobo Wambura, of Bukiroba, Musoma, recalls asking his grandmother how the mountains and trees came into being. "When you have grandchildren," his grandmother responded, "you will know how to answer that question."

Sometime later a young man, visiting relatives during vacation from school, came to Wambura's family. Inquisitive and eager to learn, Wambura listened to the stories he had to tell. When the guest withdrew to a grove of trees, the boy followed and watched as he knelt down and prayed. Later Wambura asked, "With whom were you speaking?" This young Christian, a Roman Catholic, replied that he had been talking to the God who created the mountains, the trees, and the human family.

Daniel Opanga recalls how God spoke to him through a song which he learned from a soldier, a guest of his father, Oole, the chief in Kamageta, North Mara. Again and again the man sang, "The best is still ahead . . . never again will God's people be parted." After he was gone, Opanga sang the song from time to time, wishing to know more about life beyond this world.

One day his father called him: "Opanga, I have chosen you to go away to school; then you will return and teach the others of our village."

So he was sent to live in a Seventh-day Adventist school in Kenya, where he learned the three R's and received Bible teachings. As a "reader," he tried to follow the ways of God. After he completed what this school had to offer, his father would not permit him to pursue further education.

## To the responsive, more light

The Scriptures illustrate that God always brings more light to those who respond to the light they have.[3] So with the peoples in East Lake.

Marwa Kisare had taken seriously the questions God aroused in his late childhood. Within a few years, African evangelists came and told the story of Jesus. At age 14 he began to go to church and later to school; at 21 he had completed third grade and had made the commitment of baptism. The next year, 1934, the Mennonites arrived at Shirati and with them he began to experience life in God's family; with them he met the Lord in revival. Fifty years later he recounted these experiences in his autobiography, *Kisare of Kiseru.*

Inquisitive Wambura Magesa had also wanted to know how this world came into being; how man can communicate with God. When he was grown and married, two missionaries and two local believers from Nyabangi came to his community, Kyasuki. As they sang several hymns and John Leatherman preached about the Lamb of God, Wambura's heart was touched. He recalled that from time to time the Wakiroba sacrificed a lamb to remove a curse from a village, either the curse of death or a curse occasioned by some evil deed, or sometimes to reconcile persons who were estranged. Wambura began to perceive Jesus to be the sacrifice which takes away sin and reconciles people.

Recalling other tribal customs and teachings, he realized that the Kiroba people had remnants of scriptural truths; he sensed, too, that much had been lost. Now a fuller understanding was possible because God's Book had become available. It was not long until Wambura began to follow Jesus.

As was customary, he took a new name at baptism, Yakobo.[4] During the 1947 revival, he met Jesus in a deeper experience and made some costly restitutions. In the years that followed, he encountered difficulties and opposition. While only a few Wakiroba follow Jesus, Yakobo has been a pillar of faith among them.

Opanga Oole had heard about a life beyond the present; in boarding school he began to learn the ways of God. After returning home, finding it would be easy to return to the ways of darkness, Opanga and his friend Agunya ran away to Nairobi, Kenya, and found employment. They found lodging with other youths from Kamageta, and on Sundays went with them to the Anglican Church. Opanga and Agunya entered the catechism class, commiting themselves to follow Jesus. They were baptized and confirmed, and participated in congregational life.

All the while Daniel Opanga had been developing his printing skills, both in typesetting and press operation. In 1925, after five years in the big city, word came that his father had died; he decided to return to Kamageta. Joseph Agunya went with him, and together they started worship services right there in their home community. A little congregation emerged at Alicho. Nine years later the Stauffers and Mosemanns opened Shirati Mission. Fellowship, counsel, medicines, and schooling were now available to them. Brothers and sisters from Kamageta were present in the 1942 awakening at Shirati.

## Man's rebellion absorbed by God: A meditation

From their legend one realizes that the Jita people had some profound insights into the origin and nature of man's alienation from God:

- *At the beginning God had fellowshiped with man, seeking to meet his every need.*
- *Not satisfied with what God provided, man disobeyed to get what he wanted.*
- *By attempting to control God, man upset the order of creation.*
- *There is nothing man can do to restore his relationship with God.*
- *God is still in charge on earth, reminding man of his desire for fellowship.*

The Jitas, therefore, tried to propitiate God by offering blood sacrifices, for example, a white chicken on the occasions of death or serious offenses. They made offerings to the ancestral spirits, reaching beyond themselves for a mediator who could restore relationship with God. But their offerings were ineffectual.

In contrast, the Holy Scriptures give us hope. They describe the totality of man's disobedience; they also show that, having prepared the way to return, God sought out man, confronting him, and promising reconciliation.

- *An enemy solicited Adam's loyalty, persuading him that God was keeping back some good.*
- *Refusing to be a dependent creature, Adam took affairs into his own hands.*
- *He gratified his bodily desires; he gave priority to the visible, perverting his*

*mind; he made himself a god, choosing for himself what is good and what is evil.*

- *God did not withdraw, but searched for Adam and Eve. He confronted them with their rebellion and its consequences: their sense of shame and alienation, their evasion of responsibility, travail in marriage relationships, the disciplines of hardship and of mortality (gracious restraints on the corruption and anarchy of sin).*
- *In response to faith, he covered the shame of disobedience.*
- *He removed Adam and Eve from the tree of life to ponder their helplessness; they could not make their way back.*
- *However, in judging the tempter, God had already promised that a son of the woman would crush the enemy; by absorbing the flaming sword he would open the way to the tree of life.* [5]

What the Jita did not know, like all peoples not having divine revelation, was that before creation of the universe Jesus Christ had given himself to bridge the gap between disobedient man and the Father, to establish a kingdom in which the will of God will be done on earth as it is in heaven.

*For sinful helpless man, this was Good News:*
*God himself had taken the initiative.*
*He came into our world in Jesus Christ, the second Adam.*

*Jesus offered to God a life of total obedience—*
*renouncing identity and wealth and power,*
*healing, feeding, presenting himself the way to God—*
*and as a result the disobedient hated and killed him.*

*Our Lord suffered and died, absorbing the violence,*
*bearing the full consequences of man's disobedience;*
*having thus satisfied the holiness of God,*
*he offers forgiveness.*

*Jesus swallowed up death and rose again,*
*reversing the power structures, the course of history.*
*Light overcame darkness,*
*truth triumphed over falsehood,*
*obedience swallowed up disobedience.*
*All mortals will be resurrected bodily,*

*to everlasting life or everlasting death.*
*He offers new life, here and now.*

*Our Lord ascended to heaven*
*and shares control of the universe;*
*by his Spirit he returned to earth*
*to live an obedient life in every person who submits to him.*
*He indwells disciples, forming his body—*
*the church which lives by his grace,*
*learning obedience together, helping one another keep clean.*
*Together they continue the ministries he began:*
*they bear his presence, serve human need, tell his story.*
*Through them he plants new fellowships of faith.*

*Our Lord Jesus Christ will return in power.*
*The disobedient will reap the fruit of their choices,*
*eternal separation from his presence.*
*His followers will serve him forever*
*in new heavens and a new earth.*

*All that was lost through Adam's disobedience*
*has been restored by the obedience of Christ.*
*Man is called from his disobedience*
*to join in the pilgrimage of obedience.*
*The estranged find fellowship;*
*"no people" become the "people of God."*

*God, who made possible the pilgrimage,*
*recorded the Good News in the Holy Scriptures:*
*stories, poetry, prophecies, letters—*
*the work of forty men spanning 1,500 years.*

*For 2,000 years since Pentecost*
*God has continued his initiatives—*
*searching out hungry hearts,*
*using changed persons who shared the Book.*
*He brought the good news to Marwa, Wambura, and Opanga*
*through neighbors and through strangers;*
*he united them, clusters of believers,*
*to grow together and tell the story.*[6]

# 2.

# SPECIAL MESSENGERS

### East Lake bypassed

East Lake, where Marwa, Wambura, and Opanga lived, was one of the last major areas of Tanganyika to receive resident missionaries. Lake Victoria (comparable in size to Lake Superior) became a major travel route, an easier way to Kenya and Uganda. The climate of East Lake was pleasant, and in elevations of 4-5,000 feet the malaria-bearing mosquitoes were rare. While there were the tsetse fly and sleeping sickness, they could be controlled. But in their eagerness to reach the more heavily populated, more developed areas, the early traders, and later the missionaries and explorers, bypassed East Lake. Tanganyika had been a German colony 1885-1918.

Historians believe there had been very little slave trading in the area. Fearing the Masai warriors, traders took a northern or southern route to reach the lake. Those who did penetrate the area needed the goodwill, or toleration, of the local tribes in order to survive the harshness of the journey. As for the missionaries, they went first to the larger population groups elsewhere in Tanzania, postponing approach to the dozen small groups in East Lake.

It would appear that the Seventh-day Adventists (SDA) were the first to enter East Lake, with stations at Busegwe and Majita, Musoma District, in 1909, and Utimbaru, Tarime District, in 1911. They had first arrived in Tanganyika in 1906, locating at Upare.

The Roman Catholic White Fathers established Nyegina in 1911 and Buturi (later moved to Kowak) in 1933. But they had arrived at Bukoba by 1879 and at Bukumbi, Mwanza, in 1882. The Holy Ghost Fathers had entered Bagamoyo in 1868.[1]

A Church Missionary Society (CMS) bush church was started in Kamageta in 1926. However, Alexander Mackay had already established a CMS station at Nasa in the 1870s and John Rebmann and Johana Krapf had reached Kilimanjaro and Usambara by 1848.

The last of David Livingstone's travels, 1866-73, were in or near southern Tanganyika. He and Stanley spent some time in Tabora, 300 miles south of Musoma, waiting for supplies.

An Africa Inland Mission (AIM) bush church was started at Rwanga in 1929, but in 1909 the Sywulkas had taken over the CMS station at Nasa; they had come from AIM Kenya, established before the turn of the century.

From this background one can understand why in 1934 evangelical church leaders and colonial government officials were very conscious that East Lake had been largely neglected.

### God called Mennonites

For this bypassed area God had been preparing some missionaries among the Mennonites of North America.[2] Their forefathers had fled 150 years of persecution in Europe, and in 1683 began establishing communities in eastern Pennsylvania. While they were descendants of the Anabaptist martyrs,[3] who in 1527 had commissioned one another to evangelize Europe and its colonies in the new world, persecution and the rigors of frontier life had almost extinguished their evangelistic zeal. They had largely missed out on the awakening that came through John Wesley, giving birth to the Sunday school, reforms of child labor and of prisons, the antislavery movement, foreign missions, and the Bible and tract societies.

But three generations later the Sunday schools, the camp meetings, and the Moody-Sankey revivals began to touch the Mennonites. John F. Funk and John S. Coffman, in addition to their publishing and educational ministries, introduced "Protracted Meetings," a series of evangelistic meetings with preaching in English. God raised up additional evangelists who, with Coffman, served the church from Virginia to Ontario to Kansas.[4] Young people were converted, joined Sunday schools for Bible study, and helped organize Sunday schools as a way of outreach. Hearing about the work of Livingstone and other missionaries, some of them began supporting foreign missions.

In 1882 Funk helped form an evangelizing committee, which in 1906 became the denominational board now called Mennonite Board of Missions (MBM), Elkhart, Indiana. In 1894 John H. Mellinger invited eleven Lancaster friends to a prayer meeting; from this evolved a committee, and then in 1914 the Eastern Mennonite Board of Missions and Charities (EMBMC), now at Salunga, Pennsylvania, to serve the largest concentration of Mennonite Church congregations. To promote and undergird revival, service, and missions, a denominational periodical had been launched in the 1860s and the first denominational college in the 1890s.

In response to the severe famine, the Mennonite Church (MC), the Mennonite Brethren (MB), and the General Conference Mennonites (GC) each sent missionaries to India at the turn of the century. Within a decade the MBs and the GCs had missionaries in Congo (now Zaire), and the MCs had done the exploratory work for their mission in Argentina. The Brethren in Christ sent their first missionaries to Southern Rhodesia (Zimbabwe) in 1898, and by 1906 they had missionaries in India and Northern Rhodesia (Zambia).

World War I produced a severe economic depression, and for ten years churches had to sacrifice to maintain their overseas missionaries. Nevertheless, the Mennonite Church was eager to be involved also in Africa. Offerings began to come to the denominational board at Elkhart and to the district board at Lancaster. The first contribution came to EMBMC in 1926, an amount equal to five months' wages for a working man. In 1930 a sister began sending each month the equivalent of three days' wages. Through newly awakened persons new resources were being released. The givers, however, were a minority among many who were still dragging their feet.

In a sermon in 1926 a Lancaster bishop urged EMBMC to send workers to Africa. Orie O. Miller, vice-president of the board and editor of its new periodical, *Missionary Messenger,* responded with an article helping the brotherhood think about what would be involved in acting on that vision. He collected relevant books and periodicals to be used by a churchwide committee assigned to study the needs of Africa. Then in 1929 EMBMC adopted a resolution calling on MBM, the churchwide board, to launch a mission in Africa. After studying the matter for a year, MBM responded with favorable action, but because of lack of funds, no workers were sent.

The Lancaster bishops were not satisfied. In 1930 they unanimously passed a resolution asking EMBMC to undertake such mission. They wanted their people to grow through involvement in overseas missions; they recognized that a local board could better attract workers and funds; they wanted to establish a mission that would avoid what they saw as mistakes in the first MC effort. The leaders of MBM supported this initiative with prayers and counsel. Wanting to be a part of this first MC mission in Africa, a number of churches they represent have been providing some workers and finance.

24

## A step of faith

To undertake a new mission during worldwide economic depression was a step of faith. Some persons urged that it was foolish to begin at the very time older missions were finding it necessary to reduce staff. Others, however, affirmed that the church's first responsibility is to obey the Lord Jesus, trusting him to provide for the missionaries. The offerings that had already come were God's nudge to move forward.

As the mission board weighed the matter, one brother asked how much money designated for Africa had been received. Treasurer Henry Garber named the sum in hand, a very small amount, and added: "But our God is almighty, the Lord of heaven and earth. For forty years he has provided every need of our board." A resolution to launch the new mission was adopted on April 4, 1933.

Immediately the church picked up the burden of prayer for finding suitable missionaries. Elam and Elizabeth Stauffer responded to God's call through the church. They sold their dairy and poultry farm and found other homes for their foster children. Others were called to replace them in the worker team at Miners Village Mission. Another of Elam's credentials was experience as a schoolteacher.

About the same time, John and Ruth Mosemann also accepted the call. John had worked in the family's peanut-butter business. From his father, a popular evangelist and bishop over a large circuit of congregations, he had also picked up a good understanding of church work. John was a college graduate; Ruth had also prepared for some Christian ministry. After appointment the mission board sent them to New York for a short medical course for missionaries.

During this time Merle and Sara Eshleman also sensed God's call and enrolled in medical training.

## To Africa, but where?

Although the church, the mission board, and two young couples were ready to move into Africa, no one had any idea where on that vast continent the Stauffers and Mosemanns were to go. Eager to discover God's leading, the mission board chose its vice-president, Orie Miller, to investigate with Elam Stauffer while the church united in prayer that they would find "the place the Lord has prepared." As part of their preparation, they sought information and counsel from the Philadelphia headquarters of United Presbyterian missions.

On December 2, 1953, at Weaverland church the four missionaries and Orie were commissioned by a large assembly of 1,500. Rejoicing to see this new mission initiative, these brothers and sisters were ready to give themselves to prayer and to financial support.

Buoyed by such support, Miller and Stauffer proceeded to London, where they sought the counsel of Alexander McLeish, World Dominion, and D. M. Miller, Africa Inland Mission. In Berlin they met with missionary statesman, Julius Richter. From these consultations they sensed that they should check out Sudan and Tanganyika and, as a final option, Ethiopia.

Traveling through Egypt, they proceeded to Sudan and were told about a large area still without a mission. However, it was clear that they should not come to a decision until they had made contacts in Tanganyika. By ship they entered Dar es Salaam on January 17, 1934, at the very time when mission leaders (other than Roman Catholics) had come together to organize the Tanganyika Missionary Council. These brothers directed them to consider the area to the east of Lake Victoria. When they checked with government leaders, they received the very same advice.

Thanking God, they cabled the mission board reporting guidance to Tanganyika and asking that Elizabeth Stauffer and the Mosemanns proceed to Dar es Salaam. Having in hand a letter from Mr. Miller of AIM London, Orie Miller and Elam Stauffer boarded the train to visit AIM's Tanganyika director, William Maynard, in Shinyanga, and pioneer missionaries, the Sywulkas, in Mwanza.

They were welcomed by Mr. Maynard and his wife, a medical doctor, and well received by Emil and Marie Sywulka, who had already served in Portugese East Africa, Kenya, and Tanganyika for twenty-seven years. In getting acquainted, they discovered that the Sywulkas were Defenseless Mennonites from the States. Real prayer warriors, they had been praying for additional missionaries to plant churches in the East Lake area. However, it had never occurred to them that God might send some other Mennonites. Soon Emil warmed to Elam and offered to lead him on an exploratory safari. This gave an opportunity for Orie Miller to make a side trip to visit the mission in India, where his brother was sick at the time.

Elam Stauffer began to learn more about East Africa as he assisted with safari preparations. Sywulka chose some porters and an evangelist who would visit and teach the small AIM congregations already begun south of Musoma. The party traveled by motor truck and bicycle, by sailboat and dugout canoe, and on foot. Since the rains had begun, they encountered much mud and some flooded rivers. Crossing Mara Bay from

Musoma, they proceeded to Utegi, a central location in North Mara, situated on the road to Kenya. But Chief Saronge was unwilling for another mission to be established in his chiefdom.

### On to Katuru, Shirati

They moved westward to Shirati, a tiny port on Lake Victoria, the former regional headquarters of the German colonial government. They found Chief Nyatega eager for his people to get some schooling, to learn trades, and to receive medical help. Stauffer opted for a mission plot near the lake, noting that the population was clustered there. However, Sywulka supported Nyatega's suggestion for a hilltop location, saying, "The people who want what you have to offer will come wherever you are located." They agreed on the Katuru Hill location, about two miles from the lake; the date was February 14. A few years later the missionaries studied the background of the peoples of North Mara; they were intrigued to discover that their first ministry was to a people who had come from Sudan a century earlier.

Stauffer and Sywulka returned to Musoma and made application for a right of occupancy. They traveled to Busekera, Majita, and participated in a baptismal and communion service arranged by the evangelist. Thirty-four days after they had left Mwanza, they arrived back, and Stauffer began diligent study of Swahili. With a New Testament in hand, he built on what Sywulka had taught him as they traveled.

At the end of March he returned to Dar es Salaam to welcome his wife and the Mosemanns. Meanwhile, Miller was en route from India by way of Mombasa, where he boarded the *S.S. Adolf Woermann,* on which the missionaries were traveling. Sent on their way by 450 in New York, the three were welcomed to Dar es Salaam by two Lancastrians. The five lodged in New Palace Hotel from April 3 to 6; they prayed and counseled together, formally establishing "Mennonite Mission." Elizabeth Stauffer selected Psalm 109:27 as a cablegram message to the home church: "That they may know that this is thy hand; that thou, Lord, hast done it." The five committed each other to God; Miller returned to America, and the missionaries took the train to Mwanza.

For this time of waiting, they rented a house, spending their time studying Dholuo, learning some building techniques by helping Sywulka, and buying building supplies. The Mosemanns spent a week with Doctor Maynard and her team at Kola Ndoto Hospital getting a little experience in dispensary and maternity ministries. In their prayers the four were led to ask for prompt issuance of the right of occupancy. When it came to hand in only three months, Sywulka praised God: "In all my years I never experienced so prompt issuance of an R.O.; it often takes a year."

Trunks and building supplies were loaded into two dhows with three servants looking after things. The missionaries and one lad traveled by pickup with AIM missionary Mr. Nelson to Nasa station; after a day of rest and visiting, he took them on to Musoma. There they bought more supplies, boarded the dhows, and arrived at the small Shirati pier on Saturday, May 26.

Now they had experienced the fulfillment of God's leading to the church—after seven years of prayer, counseling together, and investigation. For them, three months of travel—with many new experiences, time for prayer, and opportunities for language study—were now finished. Within two weeks of receiving the right of occupancy they had arrived at Shirati. After setting up camp in a native court building, the four Americans and four Sukuma helpers sang and prayed, praising God. That night there was a heavy rain, followed by bright moonlight.

# 3.

# ESTABLISHING BEACHHEADS 1934-42

In this chapter the history of Shirati from 1934-36 is recounted step by step, but from 1936-42 only major events will be touched upon. The four stations which followed will be described, each in the respects in which it was different from the others, each from its beginning to the 1942 revival.

## a. SHIRATI

### Arrival of the missionaries

On June 5, 1934, Kawira Nyambok was going about his usual duties, herding his father's cattle on the edge of Mkoma community. With him were friends, also looking after their fathers' herds. Although the boys were, as usual, talking and gossiping, Kawira remained alert to all that was happening. At this time there was a special freshness about him, for he had given himself to God. In his private prayers, he had made a commitment, just as he had been taught in the local Adventist school.

Kawira motioned with his arm: "Look, something is coming from the shops at Sota; what is it?" All of them watched. The German rope-maker's oxcart was approaching, loaded with trunks. Seated on top were two strangers—white women. "Who are they?" he asked his friends.

Immediately these women began waving their arms in greeting. "Where might they be going?" the boys wondered as they followed, close enough to notice the peace and joy reflected on the white faces. Soon the boys turned back to look after their cattle.

A few days later when their older brothers decided to go to Katuru to check what these strangers might be doing, the herdboys trailed along. Under a big tree they saw a shelter, a *banda,* constructed from corrugated iron sheets. With the two women were their husbands.

These youngsters peered curiously through the doorway. They saw trunks stacked to divide the banda into two rooms. The missionaries were sitting around a box on which their meal was set out. "What amazed me," said Kawira later, "was that they were eating some of the same vegetables we use at home."

The boys noticed that a portion of the hilltop had already been cleared, stones were gathered into piles, and timber and corrugated iron roofing were stacked near the shelter. Already the white men had hired a number of local persons to work with them.

### The first worship service

On Sunday, June 10, the missionaries and their four helpers from Mwanza sat together in front of the *banda* for a worship service. The next Sunday five locals joined them, for the missionaries had been inviting workmen and everyone who stopped to greet them. The Sukuma helpers introduced several Swahili hymns. Elam Stauffer taught the English chorus, "Come to Jesus," and his wife, Elizabeth, presented each person with a small picture card. In hesitant Swahili, Elam told the story depicted on one of the cards. After a closing prayer, the missionaries exchanged greetings with all who had come. That simple service was an historic event, the beginning of Mennonite worship at Shirati, another step in the church's pilgrimage.

The next day workmen began building the foundation of the first house. Some continued gathering stones while others dug the foundation. One worker experimented with making bricks from earth on the compound; some with only a little anthill dirt, others with more, and some with much. Soon the right formula was discovered and other workmen joined in making usable bricks—ones which did not crack when drying in the sun, or dissolve in the rain.

### Helping the sick

One day a workman complained of sickness, and another had hurt himself on the job. Ruth Mosemann treated both of them promptly, drawing on her training in the treatment of simple illnesses and her supply of medicines. Soon sick people were coming each day. This small ministry from the kitchen door, a "good Samaritan" response to need, gave birth to the large ministries to follow. It helped build good relations in the community.

Five weeks after beginning construction, the missionaries moved into their first house. Built of sun-dried bricks, it had a room for the Stauffers, a common room, and a room for the Mosemanns.[1]

In August Elam and John set out to choose a location for a second station near Musoma. They found a plot in Bukiroba and applied for a right of occupancy. While away from the pressure of work schedules, they talked about how to share the gospel with their workmen. When they returned, they began reading the Scriptures and praying before assigning duties.

Two weeks later visitors arrived, Robert and Kathryn Smith, their two children, and Clara Ford, missionaries among the Kuria people of Kenya. Since they were temporarily out of money, the Mennonites took them in. Smith was a builder, so Stauffer invited him to draw up plans for the first missionary dwelling. They agreed on a poured concrete structure. They went together to Kenya for supplies and Smith began the project. For four months the two missionary teams helped each other.

Also in August a thatched shelter was built, a tabernacle for worship; attendance jumped from 35 to 100 by the end of September. Because more sick people were coming, Ruth Mosemann moved her dispensary from her living room to the timber shed to facilitate examining persons and dispensing medicines.

### The opening of school
School began on October 1, four months after the opening of the station. Pastor Mosemann was in charge, and Zedekia Kisare and Koja Migire were the teachers. Each morning from seven to ten o'clock they taught children and workmen in reading, writing, arithmetic, and Bible. Each afternoon Mosemann and Miss Ford instructed the teachers—in teaching methods and Bible knowledge. The overarching goal for the school was to enable persons to read the Word of God. At this time only the New Testament was available in Luo, and the Old and New Testaments in Swahili. A few persons had a copy of the Swahili Bible prepared by the Germans. It was prized for the attractive drawings that illustrated it.

Those who attended school in the early years still remember how they enjoyed singing with Mosemann, the vigor with which he played football, and his skills in running and spear-throwing. A friendly person with a ready Luo greeting, "Misawa," he soon became known as "Bwana Misawa." Today the station is still called "Kabwana Misawa" (Mr. Hello's Place).

Because the dispensary ministry was growing, Nathanael Gomba was chosen to help Ruth Mosemann. Persons came for treatment of leprosy, syphilis, leopard wounds, large ulcers, and ordinary sicknesses. Elam Stauffer, in a report to the mission board, commented that many can be treated and that others who need special help are encouraged to go to the government hospital at Musoma, a two-day journey. Only a few went to Musoma, he reported; most refused saying, "Your God will help you." It required more effort, as Stauffer explained, to try to persuade them to go to Musoma than to try to help them with the resources available. And for such persons additional prayers were offered. Stauffer's letter concluded with a request for medical missionaries, a doctor, and a nurse.

One day when "Mama" Mosemann was sick in bed, Nathanael and his assistant, Kawira Nyambok, carried on without help, examining patients and dispensing medicines. Nathanael felt he needed a tonic. He chose a bottle which looked like the tonic Ruth had given to persons recovering from malaria. As soon as he tasted the contents, he recognized it as a poison. Fearfully, he reported what he had done. While John worked with him to induce vomiting, Ruth and a cluster of Christians prayed. Gomba was spared. Never again did he presume to use the medicines set aside to be prescribed by Ruth only.

Chief Nyatega undertook to improve the dispensary. After two small children had died of pneumonia, he sent workmen to build two huts where the critically sick could be looked after regularly by the medical staff.

### The catechism class

After seven months—it was in the Christmas worship service—opportunity was given for commitments to follow Jesus. Twenty-seven persons responded and entered the catechism class on the following Saturday. About this time women began attending the services.

Early in the new year Elam and Elizabeth Stauffer moved into the first family residence. The cost of the house, built of concrete, came to double the estimate. To spread their funds over more projects, the missionaries agreed that future dwellings would be of sun-dried bricks.

In February, forty-one enrolled for the second term of school, an encouragement to the teachers. To attract women and girls, classes were shifted to the afternoon.

Soon after this, the first pickup truck and refrigerator were brought from Kenya. While these conveniences would enable them to better serve the Africans, they also set the missionaries apart, as did their housing and education, despite their simple life in other ways.

During the first quarter of 1935 the missionaries experienced some special disciplines. At the beginning of the year Elam was near to death with malaria. In March Elizabeth experienced a miscarriage; the child was buried at Shirati. The Stauffers were given a time of rest in Mwanza.

During the month of May, Sunday school classes were organized for the children and youth. For the first time believers were given opportunity to testify in the worship service. On the very first occasion, seven persons responded with testimonies that warmed the heart. One who had been under much pressure to go to a witch doctor gave thanks for God's keeping; he had been helped by Psalm 27:1-3.

The missionaries praised God for such blessing on their limited faltering efforts. During that first year they had needed to spend much time simply providing the necessities of life, particularly housing. These duties had sapped their strength more than they realized. A visit by AIM friends, Charles and Laura Hess and children, came as a needed tonic. One evening while Hess was entertaining his children and guests with shadow pictures, the Stauffers and Mosemanns found themselves laughing again.

Language study had also been a demanding task. The Stauffers were learning Swahili, the language of government and business, while the Mosemanns concentrated on Luo, the Nilotic language of the local population. For all of them, language study required their best efforts; sometimes it brought Elizabeth Stauffer to tears and earnest prayer.

In spite of these preoccupations, the missionaries had lost no time in showing their love for the people by dispensing medicines and establishing a school. And every Saturday, together with local believers, they went to the homes of neighbors to invite them to worship services and to tell about Jesus.

Two new thrusts marked the beginning of the second year at Shirati. For women, a sewing and Bible class was started in June 1935. Now that a committed group of believers had emerged, the bringing of offerings became part of the Sunday worship.

In July Dr. Lillie Shenk and Nurse Elma Hershberger arrived; almost at once they began looking after the sick. In another three weeks when the builder couple, Clinton and Maybell Ferster, arrived, Elam and John looked forward to more time for Bible and language study.

Sensing that Bukiroba would become their central station, Stauffer realized that the plot they had asked for, and received, was too small. In August he and Ferster applied for an extension, but they were refused. They also selected a plot for a station near Mugango, but were not accepted. Two weeks later they made another approach at Bukiroba; they were granted an extension and a lakeshore garden plot.

### The first baptisms

They returned to Shirati for the first baptismal service. On September 15, 1935, fifteen persons were baptized and six were received from other denominations. Each applicant had not only made a profession of faith and completed catechetical teachings; they also were seen to have experienced a change of life. Pastor Elam Stauffer led the service on the lakeshore. After each person had given his personal testimony, the fifteen were baptized one after another. Kneeling in the water, each vowed to leave the old life and to follow Jesus until death. Then water was poured on the head, and Stauffer extended the right hand of fellowship. Zedekia Kisare stood near Stauffer and interpreted for him. As his wife, Nyaeri, was being baptized, a poisonous snake passed between them. Some saw this incident as assurance that God was founding this new church; Satan was under limitations.

Those who were baptized were Malaki Are, Eliseba Awasi Yakobo, Nathanael Gomba, Ezekiel Kachare, Zephania Koja Migire, Thadayo Makori, Samuel Ngoga, Esta Nyangi Samuel, Susana Nyaeri Zedekia, Musa Odanga, Paul Odero, Yohana Waryuba, Julia Otwandi, Simeon Otulo, and Mika Shindano. Those who were received by transfer were Zedekia Kisare, Yakobo Agwanda, Maritha Simeon, Daniel Opanga, Joseph Agunya, and Ayubu Ntemi.

In late afternoon these 21 and the eight missionaries gathered again in the tabernacle to remember our Lord in a communion service. Then they symbolized mutual submission by washing one another's feet.

As they had been taught by the missionaries, the new Christians wore a prescribed garb to show that they were people of God. The women were dressed in white dresses and a prayer covering; the men wore shorts and a shirt. The wearing of long trousers and shoes was considered worldly.

Two weeks later a strong wind blew down the tabernacle. Until a sun-dried brick meetinghouse was ready, worship services were held in the workshop. Nevertheless, Ruth Mosemann proceeded to develop the Sunday school. She arranged a class for each age group and prepared lesson outlines and some teaching aids. Those who participated remember best the singing, the hymns. Both Pastor and Mama Mosemann were excellent song leaders, and they were able to teach and converse in the local language, Luo.

October 27 was a very special day—the first Christian wedding was solemnized. Thadayo and Julia, from that first baptismal class, pledged themselves to each other for life.

On the following day Stauffer and Mosemann went to Majita to consult with Emil Sywulka who was suggesting that the Mennonites assume oversight of the AIM outschools; with such possibility in mind, they chose another site for a station at Mugango.

In December the Stauffers and Fersters moved to Bukiroba to open that station. For eighteen months the missionaries had concentrated their energies on Shirati station and its outchurches; for the last five months they had been a team of eight. The transfer of four to Bukiroba formed a second center of interest, with a third, Mugango, in prospect. And in another nine months Shirati would send six of her national leaders to the training school at Bukiroba.

## The girls' home

Relieved of responsibility in the dispensary, Ruth Mosemann gave more time to home visitation. Much of her enthusiasm and energy went into preparations for a home for girls. Already on the compound were three dormitories for boys, some of whom had come from Kenya. Some of these young believers, having as examples the faithful wives and good homes in the congregation, expressed a strong hope that they would be able to marry believers who knew how to read.

Young girls evidently felt similar urgings; several expressed their desire to follow the Lord and came to live at the mission even before the dormitory was ready. Christian women cared for them and helped them start gardens for the girls' home. Other girls promised to come as soon as the dormitory was ready. On May 12, 1936, six girls came to clean the building and surrounding area. The next day they moved in, with several other girls joining them.

Many fathers, however, insisted that religion is not for women and girls. Some brought so much pressure that a few girls left the home. Later, one for whom the other girls had diligently prayed, came back, for she had tasted genuine care and love. Some parents, who sensed that a daughter had made a firm choice to follow the ways of God, relented and gave permission for the girl to stay.

The establishment of this home was the answer to many prayers, both at Shirati and in North America. Some special offerings provided the extra finance needed. Yakobo and Eliseba Agwanda served as houseparents.

## The second baptismal service

On May 3, 1936, eleven believers were baptized and eight were received on confession of faith. One of those baptized was Nashon Kawira Nyambok, one of the cattleherders who had followed the oxcart in 1934. Out of fear of hellfire judgment, he had made a private commitment in response to teachings at school. When he heard these missionaries preach that God loved him, even enough to die for him, he sensed God confirming this love within his own heart. He made a public profession and joined the catechism class. Later he would learn the way of victory over the sins of youth.

Also in this group was Ibrahim Ogwal from Kamageta. Shortly after he had come to faith, his two children became sick and one died. His wife began to pressure him, saying that these difficulties had come because he had left the ways of the ancestors. When he realized that the whole clan was opposed to his faith, he walked fifteen miles for fellowship with Pastor Mosemann. Together they read the story of Job, noting that, though Job's wife had turned against him, God was still with him. Ibrahim was encouraged to realize that God allows faith to be tested, not to overthrow it but rather to strengthen it. Ibrahim took heart and continued firm in his commitment.[2]

After the baptismal service, 47 Christians partook of the Lord's Supper and washed one another's feet. Participating in this service were brothers and sisters from Kamageta and other outchurches.

### The meetinghouse

Before it had been used for three years, the first meetinghouse was no longer adequate to accommodate meetings involving the six outchurches. It was agreed to build a new church 84' x 28' and to use the other building for school purposes. The new meetinghouse was completed and dedicated in April 1939.

The guest preacher for the day, Ezekiel Muganda from Majita, brought a message that is still remembered: "Give no opportunity to the devil" (Eph. 4:27). He showed Satan to be as clever as the hunter of hippopotami.

When the hippo floats at the surface of the water, a harpoon is thrust into his side; it is made so that it continues to penetrate and not come out. Because the harpoon is so small, the hippo ignores it, not realizing that floats attached to it show his location. He goes about his normal pursuits, and each time he surfaces the hunter puts in another harpoon, each time with less difficulty. The wounds swell, the hippo becomes sick, and he finally dies. The carcass floats to the surface and is pulled in. Muganda underscored the fact that Satan comes at first with very small matters; then he steps up his attacks, finally separating the believer from his Lord.

Shortly after the celebrations there were changes of leadership. John and Ruth Mosemann departed on furlough and Elam and Elizabeth Stauffer, just back from the States, were assigned to Shirati. Dr. Lillie Shenk had also completed her term, and Dr. Merle Eshleman replaced her at the hospital.

Soon there were some important decisions to be made. The outbreak of World War II occasioned some concerns for the safety of the missionaries, and there were appeals to the colonial government for the recognition of conscientious objectors. The search for opportunity to expand into new areas was continued. Another question related particularly to Shirati—to what degree should the medical work be expanded? It took five years to consider the alternatives and their future implications, and to come to a decision.

**Church counselors**

The many questions the little congregation had to deal with drove the missionaries to draw upon the experience and insights of stable believers. From the beginning Zedekia Kisare and Zephania Migire helped the missionaries to learn the languages and to understand local customs. After Stauffer and Ferster moved on to Bukiroba, Mosemann involved Kisare, Migire, and others in the issues which arose. When a 1938 deputation from America affirmed the ministry of counselors and the establishment of church councils, Kisare and Migire were formally chosen to serve as elders, together with Yakobo Agwanda, Thadayo Makori, and Simeon Otulo Kisare.

On many occasions God used these elders to get to the heart of matters which completely baffled the missionaries because they did not understand the tribal culture. The main responsibility of these brothers, however, was to counsel and pray with persons facing decisions or difficulties. Even community people respected them; in fact, some persons were afraid of them. An older sister testified, "Before I really knew Jesus, I regarded them like God. When they would come to our homes, we were alarmed and afraid."

A missionary paid special tribute to their work: "The growth of the church cannot be attributed to missionaries, but rather to the hard work and prayers of the elders and evangelists. Some of the most effective ones are known only to God."

By 1942 the church at Shirati and its six outchurches had about 100 members and an attendance of 400. However, many members, even elders, were defeated in their daily lives. Others were praying for revival.

## b. BUKIROBA

### Getting started

Clinton and Maybell Ferster and Elam Stauffer moved to Bukiroba on December 4, 1935; (convalescing from malaria, Elizabeth joined them later). They had a four-hour drive to Mara Bay, a wait, and one hour on a small ferry before they arrived in Musoma. After some shopping, they drove six miles east to the Bukiroba plot, arriving early afternoon. They pitched their tent at Mchandwa hill near the village Nyabangi, named for the distinguished chief who was buried there in 1912. Near the hill was a tribal worship place. On the other side of the hill were the ruins of a once-attractive Adventist station; a German soldier who died in the 1914-18 war lies buried there.

The local chief had built two houses of light poles for the missionaries and their helpers who came with them from Shirati. In this way he showed his joy that a mission was being established among his people. But both houses still needed a roof. So the next day a temporary shelter was built. Local workmen had a roof on the one house by Sunday, so that it could be used for the worship service.

One of the helpers was Wambura Magesa, who had asked his grandmother about creation. He was eager for some education, and contributed ropes for tying the thatch. Unfortunately, soon after the school opened he had to withdraw; because thieves had stolen some of his father's cattle, he had to stay home and herd.

Every Saturday the missionaries visited the homes of their neighbors. After two months, attendance on Sundays reached forty-one, including seven women with babies. Worship began in small-group studies, their Sunday school. The children were taken to the shelter where bricks were stored; there they were taught hymns and Bible stories. Even a few older folks joined the children's group. The preaching service followed.

Home visitation and preaching began to bear fruit. The first believers were Timoteo Magoti, Stefano Magige, and Paul Magige.

### Training for leaders

John and Catharine Leatherman, who had been recruited as teachers for the leadership training school, arrived in Tanganyika in May

1936. They began language study at Shirati, and then moved to Bukiroba to open the school on October 21. All the students came from Shirati: Zedekia and Susana Kisare, Yakobo and Eliseba Agwanda, Daniel and Susana Opanga, Samuel and Esta Ngoga, Thadayo and Julia Makori, and Zephania and Rusabella Migire.

Classes for the men were mainly biblical: New Testament and Old Testament, leadership methods, and church history, all taught by John. They were also given additional basic education—the subjects covered in grade four, taught by Catharine. Her classes were interesting and helpful. After she had shown how a crawling worm later becomes a beautiful butterfly, one student exclaimed, "Here is an illustration from which one can teach the resurrection."

In time Catharine also began to help the wives by teaching Bible, sewing, health, and the care of children. Both students and teacher found great satisfaction in these classes.

Since some of the men had experience in church work, they were given some practical assignments. Zedekia and Zephania taught in the station school, a class for beginners and another for those who had made some progress in reading. They taught the usual subjects and Bible. Zephania taught the catechumens each Saturday.

In December a Wednesday prayer meeting was begun. At this time the Sunday attendance had declined. When the missionaries did some checking, they discovered that some felt they had already attained, counting themselves people of God because their names were written in a book at the mission.

In the months that followed—in 1937—some school boys made professions of faith. Nyerere Itinde emerged as one who had truly committed himself to Jesus. In contrast, others who made profession were not serious. On another occasion a group responded with raised hands to indicate readiness to follow the Lord. When John Leatherman met privately with them, he emphasized that anyone not willing to give up alcoholic beverages should leave the group. Three persons withdrew. Then he asked those who had never done any wrongs to go. All left but two, who showed serious intentions.

When the teacher training school, later called the Bible school, opened for the second year, two families from Mugango joined the class, Ezekiel and Raheri Muganda and Jona and Lea Itine. Concerned because students were having difficulty in finding foods to garnish their ugali (thick porridge), the school purchased a fishing net for their use. As a result, the families had fish for food and a little income for other needs.

### Baptisms

In October 1937 Timoteo Magoti and another were baptized. Mariamu Magoti, Stefano Magige, Simeon Magoti, and Hezekia Odera were baptized in the following year.

At this time two old women experienced the joy Jesus gives. Each had a son at home who had begun to believe, and both had assumed that following Jesus was only for youth. But the Spirit of God, who seeks to draw all men, revealed to their hungry hearts that Jesus had died for them too.

Satan stepped up his opposition lest additional persons be released. A worship service was disrupted by a demon-possessed woman shouting in Luo, though it was not her native tongue. A group of Wakiroba youth were put through circumcision rites and taught the tribal responsibilities of adults; offerings to the spirits were made on their behalf. Afterward many of this group lost interest in the Word of God. When a neighbor died, the missionaries found it difficult to comfort the widow because the deceased husband had been an unbeliever. Experiences like these weighed heavily on their hearts.

Christians and believers continued faithfully visiting their neighbors. Sometimes a missionary went with a national; sometimes two nationals went together. The local believers were very persistent. If a neighbor was not at his house, they were likely to follow him to the garden or wherever he might have gone.

In 1939 John Leatherman and Daniel Opanga took responsibility for evangelistic ministries in Musoma, which had been begun by Elam Stauffer. Leatherman obtained a plot of land and built a meetinghouse at his own expense. Within a year thirty-five persons were attending the Sunday services. Afternoon services were held in the prison. The Thursday Bible classes in the government boarding school continued to reach many boys, including the sons of chiefs and headmen.

### World War II

The Second World War both tied the missionaries to Africa and helped them hang loose. Because furloughs to North America were not possible, provisions were made for special three-month leaves in East African locations.

On the other hand, they were ready to leave Africa at a moment's notice. They were called to a meeting at Bukiroba to receive instructions from the British and American embassies and to prepare contingency plans for travel to one of the seaports, should the Germans win the conflict in East Africa. The missionaries kept their suitcases packed. At each station they counseled with the church elders, discussing pastoral care of believers and maintenance of mission stations, in the event that expatriates suddenly needed to leave.

The war brought other difficulties and challenges. Gasoline was very scarce; each station received a ration of four gallons a month. Only the most urgent trips could be undertaken.

Elam Stauffer and John Leatherman took steps seeking recognition for conscientious objectors. They approached the provincial commissioner requesting the opportunity for Mennonites to perform some alternate service. After a year and a half, the officials stopped at Shirati with their answer. Each potential Mennonite draftee was to carry a letter of identification. If called by his chief, he would be given opportunity to witness to his conscience before an official who had authority to assign alternate work or to send him to the army. Despite these arrangements, some Mennonites joined the military, attracted by the training and future job opportunities. Because the Musoma District military quota was soon filled by volunteers, the young men whose conscience did not permit them to join were never called.

**Church periodical launched**

In February 1940 John Leatherman released the first issue of *Messenger of Christ,* a small magazine to encourage believers and to give some guidance for daily living. Produced by mimeograph, it was released each second month.

At the end of 1941 the station church building was completed. Built of sun-dried bricks with a thatch roof, as was usual for such buildings, it was plastered, waterproofed, and whitewashed. Thus semi-permanent buildings were protected against the heavy rains and made attractive, but they required regular maintenance. The long low seats within were built of bricks, appropriately plastered.

From the beginning Bukiroba, as central station, received many guests. Mennonites from the other stations stopped when they went to Musoma for food and supplies. Mission and church committees usually met there. Persons traveling to Kenya, Mennonites and others, customarily slept at Bukiroba, ready to take the morning ferry.

Since the Bukiroba compound faced Mara Bay and Lake Victoria, it was easy to watch the steamers arrive at Musoma on their weekly schedules, bringing mail, food and supplies, and sometimes guests. After the war two ships arrived at Musoma each Sunday.

At all times Mara Bay was a beautiful sight. On sunny days the water shone blue, sometimes greenish, broken by whitecaps, with billowy clouds as a background. On moonlit nights it was entrancing. On cloudy days the gray sky was reflected in the water, a variety of moods. Often a sailboat moved into the scene, delivering goods to a lakeside community. Each evening fisherman went out in dugout canoes, setting their nets. Early in the morning they went back to pull them in. They returned to shore, singing as they came. One song signified they had fish to sell; another conveyed disappointment.

## c. MUGANGO

### Fruit of AIM initiatives

A cluster of churches started by Africa Inland Mission chose to become Mennonites and became the foundation for the new mission in Mugango-Majita. When the Mennonites made their first attempt to find a station plot at Mugango, the first AIM congregation was already six years old. Fifteen months later the Stauffers opened Mugango station. God had prepared the area for their ministries.

The first AIM congregation had been started in 1929 at Rwanga by evangelists Petro and Mariamu Mangaru. Some of their adherents moved to Busumi, where another church was begun in 1932. The following year other evangelists opened Busekera, Nyamuribwa, Kwikerege, and Buringa. Butata was opened in 1934. Paulo Chai Chemere and Naftali Magai Mugenyi worked along with the AIM evangelists from Sukumaland and soon became the recognized leaders.

The Mennonites' first contact with these churches occurred in February 1934 when, after choosing Shirati as the first Mennonite station, Elam Stauffer and Emil Sywulka started back to Mwanza, stopping at Busekera for a baptismal and communion service involving all the AIM congregations.

### Finding a station site

In August 1935 Stauffer and Ferster had chosen a plot at Mugango, but their application was not accepted. Later they learned that the AIM missionaries, in conference at that very time, had agreed to counsel these congregations to join the Mennonites.

Responding to Sywulka's offer of help in locating their third station, Stauffer and Mosemann met with him on October 28. After five days of searching and counseling in Mugango and Majita, they settled on the former. From Mugango they could reach both the Jita and Ruri peoples whose languages were similar. They found a satisfactory place, and Chief Marumbo Wandwi marked out the station boundaries, a more desirable location than they had chosen the first time. And the very next month a neighboring plot was assigned to a cotton ginnery, which would attract hundreds of workers into the community.

Sywulka and Stauffer agreed that from this time the Mennonites would carry responsibility for helping these little churches. As the missionaries visited the schools and made supplies available, they and the Christians would learn to know each other. Later Stauffer and Sywulka would visit each church, giving explanations and answering questions before transfer would be undertaken.

Sywulka did everything he could to help Stauffer prepare for oversight of young churches whose language he did not yet know. On July 11, 1936, Emil came to Bukiroba, and for three weeks they collaborated on a catechism and a first reader in Jita. As they worked, he gave Elam and Elizabeth a start in learning the language. He also shared in preaching services in Musoma.

On the thirty-first they began a six-day trip to visit each of the churches. They discovered a rumor that Sywulka wanted to "sell" the AIM members to the Mennonites. Patiently Sywulka again explained that the churches would receive more help from missionaries close at hand. There was "no reason for him to travel across three bodies of water" when there was a faithful leader near to them—a brother whose basic beliefs agreed with their own. Although there were many questions, open and friendly discussions marked the negotiations.

### AIM people become Mennonites

The first congregation came to its decision; they would transfer to the Mennonites. Stauffer then recorded the name of each member and of those under baptismal instruction. In its turn each congregation considered the recommendation and came to its decision. One after another the eight congregations accepted. A total of 41 Christians had been recorded. Sywulka announced that from this point onward the Mennonites would give pastoral care and direction to the congregations.

Two months later, on October 1, 1936, the Stauffers moved from Bukiroba to Mugango, 18 miles south of Musoma. They settled into a temporary *banda,* and Elam arranged for domestic help and for some clearing of the compound, with Elizabeth to keep an eye on progress.

On October 7, entrusting her and her helpers to the Lord, he traveled 15 miles to Butata to give further doctrinal teaching before receiving the AIM Christians into membership. New missionary Clyde Shenk had accepted his invitation to share the experience.

After a message there was opportunity for discussion. There were no easy answers to the questions which dealt with marriage irregularities. Because Jita marriages did not involve a bride price, they were easily broken. Could persons who had left their first partners be received into membership? Sometimes the discussion became quite vigorous, demanding an answer. When Stauffer requested more time so that he could pray, reflect further on the Scriptures, and seek counsel, the meeting almost got out of hand. An older Christian, Simeon Chikaburi, knelt and started praying. A younger man, Ezekieli Garikika, walked out and could not be persuaded to return. Elam closed the meeting.

### Evangelist Ezekiel Muganda

The following month Stauffer moved Ezekiel Muganda and his family from their home in Majita to lead the church and school at Busumi. Muganda had begun his spiritual pilgrimage with Salvation Army, Mombasa; back home he was baptized by AIM and became their leader at Bukongo, Ukerewe. He returned to Majita to help his aging father, who died within six months. His ministry at Busumi was a fruitful one. Simeon Magoti Sanjaga came to faith and became a leader in the congregation (he was still serving in 1983). Among the youth who believed were Mawawa Mabeba and Mato Sigira; they became outchurch leaders and later were ordained. Certainly Stauffer's assignment of leadership responsibilities to Muganda was a wise one. In this time of transition and questions, it demonstrated confidence in the AIM brothers and their gifts.

In December Elam returned to Majita to give more teachings. At the close he received twenty-five persons by transfer and baptized four. The group fellowshiped at the Lord's table and washed one another's feet. It would appear that this service was held on December 13.

In January 1937 Stauffer worked with Ferster to help complete the first residence. However, they took three days for a trip to consult with Sywulka on how to be helpful to those caught in marriage irregularities. The station school was opened in February. On March 14, three believers were received from AIM, and two were baptized. Then Stauffer and Ferster visited the Majita churches, preaching and serving communion.

In June they and their wives were guests in the annual conference of AIM missionaries. Their special guest, Mr. D. M. Miller, AIM General

Secretary from London, brought messages and gave counsel and encouragement. The Mennonites began to wish that Lancaster leaders would come to visit them and experience at firsthand the joys and difficulties of preaching the gospel.

Soon there were problems in the Majita congregations. However, the churches were strengthened when persons involved responded to warnings and repented.

In December Phebe Yoder arrived, a new missionary nurse who was also a qualified teacher. With a vision for educational ministries, Phebe would become deeply involved in the ferment which called for the registration of Mennonite schools. Just before her arrival the government had announced that only graduates of accredited schools could proceed to higher levels of education. The religiously oriented mission schools did not qualify. Phebe's first Christmas included a wedding—of Jona I. Mirari and Lea Makongoro—in the partially completed station meetinghouse.

New missionaries, Ray and Miriam Wenger, arrived in April 1938. As was customary, they visited each station and then plunged into language study, for it was apparent that they would need to take the leadership of Mugango-Majita within the year.

## Deputation from America

The year 1938 saw some important events, including a visit from Lancaster Conference representatives and a bishop ordination. In June the missionaries welcomed the deputation—Bishop Henry Lutz, representing the Lancaster bishops, and Henry Garber from the mission board. Garber's wife came with him for a visit with their daughter and son-in-law, John and Catharine Leatherman, and their granddaughter Lois.

The visitors wanted to observe, to encourage, and to give counsel to the missionaries. They also wanted to get acquainted with the believers and to encourage their leaders, expecting to learn much and to be strengthened in faith through the fellowship. They were also commissioned by the church at home to find potential places for expansion within Tanganyika and to explore the possibility of starting a new mission in another African country.

The delegation spent time on each of the stations; they also visited some of the brothers and sisters of AIM, particularly at Kola Ndoto Hospital, 200 miles to the southeast. While there, Henry Lutz became ill with malaria. After he returned to Bukiroba, he experienced a relapse which delayed their journey home.

The missionaries met at Bukiroba from August 30 to September 2 for final consultations with the deputation—meetings which included rewriting the mission constitution.

As a result of their observations, the deputation was ready to affirm the missionaries in many ways. They supported the practice of seeking counsel from mature believers and of involving them in preaching. They affirmed that each congregation choose elders to share in local leadership, and that each year elders from all stations should meet together in a general church council. In this way they would learn to know each other, to seek God's guidance together, and to make decisions on matters that affect the whole church.

## The first and the second bishops

The final ministry of the deputation was to give leadership to the choice of a bishop. On Monday, September 5, 1938, the missionaries, given opportunity to submit names to Brother Lutz, nominated Elam Stauffer and John Mosemann. Missionaries and national Christians joined in fervent prayer asking God to reveal his choice. In the traditional Lancaster Conference way, Bishop Lutz cast the lot using Bibles; the card symbolizing the call was found in Stauffer's Bible. Elam knelt and, by the laying on of hands and prayer, was commissioned as overseer of the Mennonite churches. Bishop Lutz, out of bed for the first time following his long illness, had been given strength to lead the service.

Ten days later the deputation began their homeward journey. Soon after, Elam and Elizabeth Stauffer packed their trunks, shared in the dedication of the Mugango church building, and departed on their first furlough.

Ministries to women and girls at Mugango were begun in 1939. A sewing class was established in January; later the group chose to concentrate on Bible study. In October three girls came asking to live at the mission and be taught the ways of God. Rebeka Mtemwa of Busumi was called to be matron, and a home for girls was started.

Efforts in 1940 were focused on the preparation of Jita literature. Ray and Miriam Wenger and Phebe Yoder teamed with linguists of AIM and SDA, checking a translation of the New Testament. They also worked with AIM in preparing a hymnbook. Within a year the hymnbook was available, but it was three years until the Jita Testament was published. To have a hymnbook and a major portion of the Scriptures in their mother tongue was a great joy to the believers.

When Elam and Elizabeth Stauffer returned from furlough in 1939, they were assigned to Shirati to give leadership to that growing district. Soon it was clear that he could not give adequate leadership to all the churches, and everyone agreed that it would be better stewardship of resources and improve oversight to have a bishop on each side of the Mara River. On Sunday, April 24, 1941, Ray Wenger was ordained as bishop of South Mara, responsible for Mugango-Majita, Bukiroba, and Bumangi.

Happily, he already had a strong colaborer on the station, Ezekiel Muganda. After completing Bible school in 1939 and leading Butata outchurch for one year, Ezekiel had been brought to help at Mugango.

In response to local demand, in 1942 steps were taken to open a dispensary on Mugango station. At this point the station was responsible for twelve outchurches.

## d. BUMANGI

### Community opposition
The fourth main area that Mennonites moved into was Bumangi, eighteen miles southeast of Bukiroba. In May 1937 Clinton and Maybell Ferster and Clyde and Alta Shenk began the difficult task of entering Zanaki land with the gospel.

Chief Chabwasi Sang'e had responded favorably to the missionaries' request for a plot of land and was ready to mark the boundaries. Some of his advisers, however, manipulated him so that he gave part of Kyasamiti hill, where there were so many termites that local people did not build on it. Some of the Zanakis also tried underhandedly to have the permission withdrawn so that the missionaries would have to leave, and the tribal way of life could continue uninterrupted. It was clear that preaching the gospel at Bumangi would not be easy.

The Zanaki people understood that the gospel changes lives. They feared that their daughters who accepted the Christian faith would no longer accept customary tribal marriages. They would even refuse the tribal rites preparatory to marriage. In such case the children who would be born would be regarded by the tribe as illegitimate. Customarily such children were killed to avert a curse on a whole village. Fear that their traditions might be changed made the local populace very strong in their opposition to Christianity. The pioneer missionary, Shenk, was hated intensely by tribal loyalists; at one point he was charged in the local court for upsetting Zanaki customs.

Helping the missionaries to face the situation were Jonathan Nyamhagata, an interpreter who taught them Zanaki culture and customs, and Jona Itine Mirari, a carpenter and evangelist. Jonathan had been introduced to the Lord through the Salvation Army while he was employed in City Hall, Nairobi. Serious illness had brought him back to Bumangi. Jona, the second Zanaki helper, had come to faith in Musoma and was baptized at Mugango.

One day Jona went to find poles to make a bed. Finding some suitable ones, he began to cut them, not realizing that this particular clump of trees was a place of tribal worship. Out of fear the people who lived nearby warned him. He told them that he would call Pastor Shenk who "is not afraid of your gods." With faith winning over trepidation, Jona and Clyde went back the next day, cut as many poles as they needed, put them on their shoulders and went home. The following day thirty women, each clothed in the skin of a wildebeast, surrounded the Shenk house. With a wildebeast beard crowning each head and a long cane in hand, they sang, placing a curse of death or insanity on the missionaries and on Jona.

At another place there were certain stones, regarded as sacred and used in worship. The people believed that, should they ever be moved, the stones would return to their places. Two young men, Nyakitumo Meso and Marabe Wandiba, confidently moved the stones to another location. The local people were very uneasy about this, but they later confirmed that the stones had not returned.

In all of this God protected his servants. Clyde, Jona, Nyakitumo, and Marabe continued to praise God and to speak about him. Although Satan made severe attacks on them, particularly on Jona, some believed.[3] A young man who saw the trees being cut, impressed with God's protection for his people, began to believe in Jesus.

### Changed lives

Although some in the community were impressed by the Christians' lack of fear, an even greater witness was given by the lives that had been changed. After only six months forty-five persons had indicated that they wanted to follow Jesus. The missionaries were much in prayer, realizing that most of the people were seeking only to improve their material lives. They were encouraged, however, when one man went to another to pay for a chicken he had stolen.

The missionaries announced a day for opening school, telling interested persons to come at 2:30 p.m. That morning, the Shenks found a young boy at their door at 7:30. Nyakitumo Meso's father had earlier begun arrangements for him to study at Busegwe mission, but had died before matters were finalized. So the boy had come on his own initiative, and eagerly applied himself to the lessons.

Moved by Clyde's preaching, he began to hear God speak to him. While he looked after the family herds, the voice of God followed him: "Come to me, all who labor and are heavy-laden"; "All who are in the tombs will hear his voice, and come forth, those who have done good, to the resurrection of life, and those who have done evil, to the resurrection of judgment."

One day without hesitation he responded to the invitation; he stood in the congregation confessing his sins. Believing that in his death Jesus had carried all these sins, he knew he was now forgiven. When he told this experience to his family, he was not deterred by their resistance and laughter. Soon they began to see changes in his life.

Isomba Tingayi was another youth who came to faith soon after the station was established. He had lost his father and, as the eldest son now in charge of the family, he moved their village near to the mission so that he and his younger brothers could go to school. Isomba was one who made a complete break with the past and continued steadfast; he never backslid, though the pressures of tribal customs were strong, especially at the time of his marriage.

### Resisting the powers of darkness

For his bride Isomba had chosen a Bumangi girl, Muse, who had shown that she, too, wanted to follow the Lord. His clan made the appropriate arrangements, including payment of bride price. Both clans insisted on participation in the tribal religious ceremonies associated with marriage. However, because of their commitment to Jesus both Isomba and Muse refused to compromise their faith, standing firm in spite of threats. God blessed their marriage, and when the time approached for delivery of their first child, they went to Shirati hospital to make sure that the child would not be killed at birth. When they returned home with their beautiful daughter, colonial government officers gave stern warnings to both clans, and the child was not harmed. Isomba and Muse were blessed with additional children.

The first girl to come to faith at Bumangi was Wasatu Togoro. Her warm testimony attracted other girls, including Wakuru, who left home to live at the mission. One day family members caught her, beat her, and fastened her feet with iron bands so that she could not run away again.

Seeking to show that she loved her parents, she dragged herself to the grinding stone and prepared a day's supply of porridge meal. In time she was released, although the opposition continued. Nyakitumo made approaches to marry her and arranged for her to go to Mugango girls' home for several years. When they were married and had their first child, Wakuru's mother feared to hold the baby because the parents had rejected tribal ceremonies. Only after the third child was born did she have a change of heart. When she asked forgiveness, Wakuru said, "I forgave you from the beginning. You did not understand." And the Zanaki people began to say, "If you want many children, follow the ways of the mission."

In this extended conflict, it was God who won. Second-generation Christians have testified: "What was not possible by human effort, God has accomplished. The message Shenk brought was not something he himself originated; it was from the Lord." A teacher-pastor, giving thanks for Clyde and Alta's ministry, wrote: "Their testimony grew out of their deeds and their faith."

The conflict had been difficult. The times of testing were relieved by times of rejoicing. The first evangelistic trip to Ngoreme had been undertaken in 1938. In the same year the station church building was completed and formally dedicated in October with remarkable attendance— 475 persons.

However, in 1939 there was increased opposition. As the Zanakis saw people responding to the gospel, they became more insistent about their tribal customs. Believing that faithful observance of these customs would guarantee a good life, they regarded Christianity as strange European innovations that would destroy the Zanaki ways. In an attempt to overcome the opposition, Alta Shenk made special efforts to help the women and to learn to know them. She began a sewing class. After six months 24 women and 10 children were attending. These contacts at the mission influenced them to begin attending worship services.

### Commitment to God and church

Several important events took place at Bumangi in 1940. In the first baptismal service for believers, Zakaria Magigi Mahuka, Danieli Z. Mahuka, Samson M. Nyanduga, and Lea Jona publicly committed themselves to follow Jesus, and to accountability to brothers and sisters.

In July when this small congregation hosted the first spiritual life conference for all the churches, they experienced the fellowship of the new tribe of which they were now a part. God's people came from

50

Shirati, Bukiroba, and Mugango-Majita. The conference included periods of instruction from the Scriptures and times for testimony. There was the informal fellowship at mealtimes and while camping together on the station for several days. For everyone it was a time of spiritual uplift and of making new friends.

In August the missionaries returned to Bumangi for their annual meeting. For two days they shared in worship and Bible study, and two days were spent on mission business. The major agenda item that year was a review of their basic guidelines. For more than a year they had been struggling as to how to respond to the church elders' two requests: more education and more money. The elders, who had tasted the joys of learning and its benefits, were insistent in their request for more education. They also asked for more financial remuneration for their work. It seemed to them that the missionaries relaxed when people responded to the gospel message; on the economic level they would leave the new Christians where they found them. Along with spiritual blessings, the elders wanted a better standard of living for their families.

The sympathies of the missionaries were pulled both ways. They wanted a better life for their people; they were also eager that the church be self-supporting from the very beginning. However, they also thought of other lands where the young churches were overshadowed by big schools and large medical programs, and they recalled warnings the mission board had given on these matters. They were firmly convinced of the rightness of the board's goal: to establish churches which from the beginning would share in preaching the gospel, would govern themselves, and would support their leaders. Seeing themselves hemmed in on both sides, the missionaries gave themselves afresh to the Lord, trusting him to build his church and to help them find answers.

Throughout the next year, station activities continued as usual. In 1942 Stefano Tingayi and others were baptized. In February the church was struck by lightning and burned. Promptly the believers began to repair the building. This event proved to be something of a harbinger of the fire of revival which would touch Bukiroba and Mugango the following month; by August God had begun his work in all the congregations, burning out the stubble and requiring some restructuring.

## e. NYABASI

### Converting a fort

The first missionaries in the Nyabasi area met with a warmer response than the Shenks had received in Bumangi. "Bwana Nyarero" was one of the names given to the first Mennonite missionary among the Kurya people of Nyabasi land. On January 1, 1940, Clinton and Maybell Ferster pitched their tent beneath a large tree on Nyarero hill, on the compound marked out for them by Chief Mahende Masero. Around the perimeter of the hilltop was a wall of stone. This had been one of the fortified areas before the colonial authorities had ended intertribal warfare. During Masai raids, people had come with their herds, seeking refuge. Now right at hand was a good supply of building stones, ready for use.

After two weeks Clinton and Maybell moved into a mud and wattle house. He had already built a house for the helpers who had come with him, a cook and mason and carpenter. As overseer he chose a local person, Samuel Maitarya, who had been a guide to those choosing the compound. Samuel and Eunice were Adventist Christians.

Again the mission buildings were to be of the usual semi-permanent construction. But preparations were different here from those on the earlier stations. Water had to be carried from the valley to the hilltop; bricks made from the heavy clay cracked as they dried. After experimenting with a variety of mixtures, Ferster was able to produce bricks which he could use.

Nyabasi was the fifth station for the Mennonites, opened in their sixth year of work. Reflecting on this in later years, some early Christians paid tribute to "the fire of God in them."

### The ministry of Doctor Mack

The first missionary residence was ready by June, and Noah, Muriel, and Mary Lois Mack moved into it. After some language study at Bukiroba, they had lived at Shirati, where Dr. Mack gained a bit of experience in the illnesses common to East Africa.

In July he opened the Nyabasi dispensary. From the thirty-nine people who came to him that first day, he gained an impression of the local health situation; he was touched with the confidence people were ready to place in him. Government medical officers had expressed reservations as to whether a dispensary at Nyabasi could be justified. In due time their questions were silenced by the excellent medical services provided at Shirati and Nyabasi. In fact, Tanganyika authorities deferred the establishment of a government hospital in Tarime until districts having even fewer facilities had been provided for.

The Kurya people really appreciated Dr. Mack because he visited in their homes, even as far as Bwiregi, giving medical treatment as the occasion might call for it. They had a lot of fun with a riddle he put to them: "I planted beans; I harvested meat." He could explain that his first garden was spoiled by predator animals, but with his gun he got eight rabbits and twelve small gazelles. Evidence that he is well remembered are the seven men, born during the years he served, who bear the name "Meki."

In the building work and in treating the sick, the missionaries bore witness to Jesus. And God blessed them with some fruit in the very first year. Samuel and Eunice Maitarya expressed readiness to transfer their membership, and on November 17 they were received together with a Brother Josiah. Two others, Musamba and Maswe, had begun to believe, and in March 1941 Wambura Mwita entered catechism with them. All of these persons had begun as workmen on the station.

### Strengthening Christian homes

Muriel Mack began to teach the women to read as a step in establishing strong Christian homes. In the local culture women were at the bottom of the totem pole, and all household responsibilities fell to them. Any woman who wanted to follow the Lord had to be firm in her decision and willing to work hard, for she had chosen a path different from the others in the village. When she went to a class, all her family duties would wait until she returned. If she was really going to learn to read, she would need to stick with the class, not a month but a year.

Soon the Lord of the harvest added to the worker group. Simeon and Edna Hurst arrived in December, spent six months in language study, and then moved to Nyarero. They were quickly recognized as a husband-and-wife team, working together in all they undertook, and as persons of prayer. Diligent evangelists and faithful in giving pastoral care, they were committed to visiting people, Edna carrying with her a few simple remedies to help the sick.

### Evangelist Nathanael Nyamare

The following year the Lord brought Nathanael Rhobi Nyamare and his wife, Dina, back to their homeland. As a youth Rhobi had crossed the Serengeti and trained as a teacher in the Lutheran college at Marangu. In 1929 he had put his trust in Jesus and in time was baptized. For a period he taught in the Lutheran schools. In 1939 he was transferred to a government school in Mwanza and later to Musoma, where he helped establish the Mennonite congregation.

Because of his health he was transferred to Nyarero, where he began teaching adults; then he was assigned to first and second grades in the station school. He was diligent in sharing the Word with the inpatients at the dispensary, and every weekend he went out preaching. After he started regular worship at Bukira (Kyoruba), he stayed two additional days, teaching the three R's. He was instrumental in starting churches in several communities.

Nathanael and Dina gave excellent leadership to their family. They dedicated their firstborn child to the Lord. In gratitude for God's blessings, they prayed as a family three times a day. In teaching his children, he did not hesitate to recount his own mistakes and to tell how God had helped him. In all of this God was preparing him for ministry as a pastor.

In July 1942 the station meetinghouse was dedicated. It had been built, as those on the other stations, by the labor and offerings of the local believers and the missionaries. Pupils in the school helped too, particularly by bringing grass for the thatch roof. All the missionaries were present in this service since they were on the station for their annual meeting.

Two days later many brothers and sisters gathered for the annual spiritual life conference of the total church. In this meeting many persons found spiritual help, and a revival that had begun at Mugango touched others—a revival that would spread throughout the church.

Wambura Mwita remembers with joy how he met the Lord in a new way in those meetings; however, his baptism was delayed because he had not yet learned how to read. The first baptisms at Nyabasi occurred in early 1943 when Danieli Musamba and Hezekia Maswe were baptized.

# 4.

# DEFEAT TURNED TO VICTORY, 1942

### Prayers for revival

In December 1940 Elam Stauffer wrote to a group of prayer helpers in America: "Since many among us are not enjoying the blessings of the Lord, it is evident that they are sick at heart; Shirati needs more prayer helpers so that the church be cleansed and receive the blessings of God."

Throughout the congregations joy and peace were lacking. Physical illnesses and daily distresses drained people spiritually; whereas, when love was warm and fresh, the same experiences moved them closer to the Lord. Many left the faith. For example, at Bukiroba one turned back to his sins, another was shown to be a hypocrite; finally, all the members were under discipline. In each congregation those who loved God prayed for revival, searching their own hearts.

The missionaries also experienced much heaviness. The joy of working in a new situation, of exciting experiences, had passed; life had deteriorated to mere routines. Weakened physically by the pressure of duties and bouts of malaria, they were slack in spirit. Instead of real joy there was surface frivolity. Strained relationships and some backbiting replaced the former harmony. Satan attacked some with powerful temptations; others found it hard to pray. In fact, for several years they had been praying for revival. The root of the problem was that each person, missionary and national, saw only other persons who needed revival, not the needs of his own heart.

Both church elders and missionaries lamented the fact that while 200 persons had been baptized, half had already returned to their sinful ways. And they themselves were clashing in their relationships. Now and again the elders demanded opportunities for more education and subsidy from America for their financial allowances. In the 1941 conference of all the elders, matters came to a head. Stating that they were not willing to discuss any of the issues at hand until their wages were increased, the elders walked out of the meeting. The missionaries went to their knees and sought the face of God. During this time the elders also did some praying. Later in the day the joint meeting was resumed; from the prayers and discussion came an agreement to begin teaching the tithe in the congregations. Not only would that practice teach the joy of giving; it would also provide some additional support for the elders.

## Harbingers of blessing

God heard the prayers for revival. He moved among his people seeking those who would respond. In May 1941 at Shirati, the Spirit had been dealing with a national brother. He went to Bishop Stauffer and confessed thievery, lying, fighting, lust, impure conversation, a contrary spirit, cheating in his work—he named twenty sins. Stauffer showed him God's promise of forgiveness and prayed with him; he counseled that he be prompt in obedience should the Spirit show him additional sins. In a few hours the brother was back. Again the next day he made further confessions, acknowledging that he deserved God's judgment. Again they read the promises. The brother responded, "I am truly sorry for my offenses against God; now I have peace and joy; I have been forgiven."

He requested opportunity to give his testimony in the weekly prayer meeting. That afternoon he left school early for a quiet time to prepare his own heart. He spoke with tears, recounting how he had put our Lord to shame; he praised God for forgiveness, for planting him on the rock, for giving him a new song. People listened intently. Within a few hours others came, confessing sins they had hidden and finding release.

There emerged a cluster of believers who radiated the joy of the Lord; they came to each meeting hungry for the Word. In them God made visible the blessings that come to those who repent. Of course there were some who made confessions because it appeared to be the thing to do; they were promptly warned to repent.

Many others throughout East Africa had been praying for revival. God found responsive hearts among some AIM missionaries, released them from bondages, and gave them new power in his Spirit. Hungry for such blessings, Elam and Elizabeth Stauffer attended the 1941 conference of AIM Tanganyika missionaries. God asked Elam to take a new step of personal obedience, giving him a taste of revival. While he did not realize it at the time, it was the first step of release from the paralyzing fear of repeating what were regarded as the mistakes of India Mennonite Mission. Back home they shared their experiences. With hungry hearts, they and others prayed more earnestly, culminating in a day of fasting and prayer at Shirati, January 26, 1942.

Then God stretched forth his arm among Mennonite missionaries. In March 1942 a brother revealed a deep need in his life, confessing lust and improper behavior. His fellow missionaries—shocked—regretted that they had not sensed his need and been able to help him. A husband and wife, convicted of a deep need in their lives, privately poured out their hearts in a new commitment. They began to taste revival. At Mugango some brothers were also touched; in repentance they found new life. To give the missionary brother opportunity to grow in his experience, the board arranged that he and his family return to America.[1]

## Awakening in Mugango-Majita, May

Two months later, in May, God brought a special messenger, Rebeka Mukura, to the Mugango-Majita churches. Rebeka, who in 1983 was still living and witnessing, had met the Lord and made a deep commitment to him. Illiterate, she prayed for ability to read the Scriptures. God granted her request, and she was able to read in personal devotions. Wherever she went she spoke up for Jesus. As she prayed, the Lord gave her discernment of the specific needs of persons to whom she was talking. With some AIM colleagues, she had been praying for revival among the Mennonites. One day when they arose from prayer, she found a letter from Ray Wenger inviting her to come to Mugango and share from the Word and her testimony. She was soon on her way.

Measured by normal expectations, she was a weak speaker. Her ministry was one of prayer; she could discern where God was working. Then she responded in faith, praying that his will be accomplished in the given situation.

To the church elders she was a stumbling block: "What can she teach us; she doesn't even know how to read!" (In meetings she would call out the reference, asking someone to read the Scripture portion she wanted to use.) They continued: "What is more, it is contrary to the Bible for a woman to preach! She may lead us astray."

Rebeka was not fazed by their opposition. She warned Ezekiel Muganda regarding sin in his life and urged him to repent. A number of persons were helped, including Paulo Chai and Simeon Magoti. Teaming up with her in prayer, Ray, Miriam, and Phebe were strengthened in commitment and faith.

The meetings were closed to prepare to go to Butata, Majita. Since Ray Wenger, mission treasurer, was scheduled to meet with his fellow officers, Phebe Yoder was chosen to travel with Rebeka. Because of the war, gasoline was scarce and they traveled by foot. A group from

Mugango, men and women, went along to share in the meetings.

In the executive meeting Ray Wenger and his colleagues prayed that Ezekiel Muganda would be prevented from going to Majita lest he hinder the work of the Lord. However, Rebeka and Phebe were praying that he would attend and be further helped.

Ezekiel arrived, and in the Butata meetings he met the Lord in a new way; he fell, appeared unconscious, and was carried into the tent outside. From this time onward his life was completely changed. Often he would praise Jesus for saving him, naming his sins, a testimony that touched other hearts. He learned that whenever he came short in his walk of faith—for Satan attacked him in many ways—prompt repentance brought immediate refreshment of spirit.

After three days Rebeka and the team traveled to Nyamuribwa and then went on to hold meetings in each of the Majita churches. Many experienced cleansing of life. Simeon Magoti remembers, "We confessed all our offenses." Some came to faith for the first time. Ray and Miriam and Phebe wrote to their prayer helpers, "May God be praised for his work."

Hearing of this outpouring of blessing, a small group at Shirati began to meet for prayers each morning at 5:30 a.m. Following this lead, a small group on each station met early to pray for revival.

In July Ray and Miriam Wenger and Clyde and Alta Shenk attended AIM missionary conference to share in what the Lord was doing among them. A group joined in prayer on behalf of the Mennonite conferences that would follow in a few days and for Emil Sywulka and Metusela Chagu, the speakers.

### Revival at Nyabasi, July

Three days later the Mennonite missionaries met at Nyabasi. In daytime sessions Sywulka taught from the Scriptures, and each evening he led a prayer meeting. He was preparing the group for spiritual warfare. He started with what they already believed—that because Christ died and rose, each person who responds, repenting of sins and receiving Jesus, is forgiven. He went on to emphasize the second side of the coin—that in God's provision believers have died and been resurrected together with Christ; therefore, he who will respond by renouncing fleshly desires and obeying the Savior, will experience the indwelling of Jesus. Through him Jesus will be present in the human situation, serving the needs of men and witnessing to God's love, waging battle with Satan.

The missionaries humbled themselves, confessing specific offenses, sins of omission and wrong attitudes. Sywulka exulted in the Lord as the Spirit worked. Rhoda Wenger, who had been suffering from chronic illness, was healed by prayer and anointing.

The missionaries closed their meeting on Tuesday to prepare for the churchwide spiritual life conference to follow. Many national brothers and sisters had arrived, including some who had walked four days. A Kurya youth, who in a dream saw them coming, met the group in the way and welcomed them. This experience encouraged them to believe that God had prepared special blessings.

Metusela Chagu brought most of the messages, assisted by Sywulka. They lifted up the Lord, calling people to receive forgiveness and new life. Brothers and sisters from Mugango and Majita testified that God had awakened them. In each session people were encouraged to go alone or in small groups for prayer and self-examination. Many met the Lord and made a break with sin, some in a deeper experience and others receiving him for the first time. Many prayers were offered for the cleansing of the church.

Unity in the spirit characterized the business session of the elders; it was agreed to institute the ban for those excommunicated from the church and to discipline youth who participated in puberty rites. As the groups went back to their stations, they sang and recounted the new blessings they had experienced.

Back home they shared their testimonies, and persons who had not been able to go to Nyabasi were helped. One of the roots of revival at Bumangi was the testimonies of Zakaria Magige and the schoolboys. The youth held a meeting each night in their dormitory village, singing and telling how they had been changed.

The Nyabasi experience brought new liberty into morning prayers at Shirati. They called for their seven congregations to meet on the station August 8 and 9 for a spiritual life conference and communion. They had agreed, however, that baptisms be delayed until the churches experience cleansing.

## God came down at Shirati, August

In the Saturday meetings Elam Stauffer did most of the preaching, with Zedekia Kisare interpreting. Messages were given in the power of the Spirit, with a burden that people be delivered.

On Sunday the work of the general church council was presented, and members pledged themselves to observe the ban. In the preparatory service, all present expressed readiness for the Lord's table. The leaders, however, knew otherwise. After the meeting Stauffer visited a member who was known to be hiding sin. Because the person again claimed to be ready, Stauffer and Kisare agreed to postpone the communion service.

When the congregation met again at 3:30 for communion, the postponement was announced. Hezekia Adera began to speak: "You claim that Jesus Christ is your Savior, but you are still walking in the ways of sin! If you do not allow Jesus to change you, to whom will you turn?" A few persons withdrew to pray for the meeting.

After a short message, Hezekia called the congregation to kneel in prayer. People began to pray, pleading simultaneously in low voices. As the burden of prayer increased, voices grew louder. Like a soft breeze, the Spirit hovered over the meeting. Sinners began to weep like bereaved persons, and to pray. Those who knew God began to praise, "Aleluya." A heathen woman ran from the meeting crying, "Why are you throwing stones at me?" A few others left with her. Some outsiders hurried to the church to see what was happening.

Stauffer breathed a prayer that Satan have no opportunity to sidetrack what God was doing. He began to sing, "How sweet the name of Jesus sounds," and a few joined him. As everyone came to attention, he divided people into four groups—the girls, the women, the youth, and the men—placing leaders over each. In these groups, confession followed confession like a flood, each person impatient to get rid of his sins. The leaders simply listened, except for an occasional rebuke to someone who was obviously imitating. At 7:30 p.m. the groups came together again to praise God in song and testimony. It was a time of great joy, a foretaste of heaven. At 8:00 p.m. they committed each other to God in prayer and went to their homes.

The joy of revival continued the next morning as believers met again in their early prayer meeting. Work on the station was canceled for the day. People spent their time in prayer, in paying debts, and in seeking out backsliders. Under conviction, a schoolgirl started to run away; in the path she encountered believers who warned her, and she repented. Some persons who came for medical care were touched by the Spirit and repented. Each afternoon that week there was a meeting to praise God together and to help seekers.

The following week Stauffer and a small team went to Alicho, preaching and counseling. Then they went on to Migeko and Kirongwe. "After three weeks the battle is still on," Elam reported on his return, "but it is such a release simply to follow the Spirit; for too long we tried to guide matters, expecting the Lord to bless what we undertake."

60

## The testimonies of Nyambok and Kisare

Thirty years later Nashon Nyambok reflected on what happened to him in 1942:

> This was the day when God revealed himself to me—when I repented of the sins I had hidden. Not allowing shame to hold me back, I confessed everything. Then God gave me joy, boldness, strength and freedom; he was very near to me.
>
> I needed to ask forgiveness of persons whom I had wronged and to make payment to those from whom I had stolen. I needed to correct some lies I had told, some I had acted. My spirit was celebrating; God had given me joy that brought tears. I realized how very precious is faith in Christ; I knew that I was saved. But Hezekia Adera lost out.

Bishop Kisare has also written how deeply the Lord penetrated his spirit:

> I was like a signboard which shows the way, but never takes a step in that direction. I was telling people that Jesus is the way to heaven, but I myself had not yet met the Lord; I had not recognized my sins.
>
> I had not yet repented, I had not yet confessed my sins before people. I had no assurance of forgiveness. I could not witness to the gospel because, like a sickness, sin was still operative in my body, robbing me of joy and freedom in my preaching. I was like Naaman with a bleeding leprosy hidden beneath beautiful garments, in my case, a leadership position.
>
> I had been preaching in the church, but within I was full of anger, hatred, backbiting, and shameful lusts. I was not free to take my wife with me when I traveled; I could not get along with her at home. And I could not at all get along with the missionaries. I regarded them as proud people, seeing themselves as important overlords and me as an ordinary black man; that they considered their disrespect for me to be fully justified. But Jesus did not leave me.
>
> Finally with many tears I cried out to God. And then I realized that my fellow leaders were right there beside me, seeking God also. With deep sorrow we began to ask forgiveness of each other for the terrible sins we had committed. From this point onward I have had good fellowship with my brothers.
>
> After many had repented and made confession, our wailing ceased and, by God's grace, we began to sing his praises. Faces were shining; joy and laughter broke forth, heaviness and regrets were gone. It was the first

time I had experienced anything like this!—because it was the first time I had repented of sin.

The blessings of heaven were poured out that day, for Jesus himself had visited our church! People began to declare openly where they stood before God; previously they could not do so, but now they had seen the Invisible One. Some returned things they had stolen. From this point onward people made a complete break with worldly affairs that had bound them in lives of wickedness. Some repented of witchcraft, others of repeated fornication and tribalism. We praised God for saving us from the power of darkness, from the control of Satan.

Our church had been like a small canoe in the open sea, driven by a powerful wind and sinking! If God had not come down, I don't know what we could have done for this little church. Again and again, I praise our Lord Jesus Christ for coming down to us and restoring what had been spoiled.

The missionaries also experienced a new awakening. Many times they had prayed that the Africans be revived, and they rejoiced in all that the Spirit had accomplished. But some of them, who had seen themselves to be "good," began to recognize needs in their own hearts. They admitted that the Spirit was not overflowing in their lives; they wished for more power in prayer. When they began to take God seriously, he showed them sins of hypocrisy, pride, hardness of spirit, self-seeking, lording over others, judging others, lack of love—truly a terrible list. As they repented, turning afresh to Jesus, new life began to flow out to others.

Some years later the late Andrea Mabeba told John and Catharine Leatherman, "When we church leaders are together fellowshiping around the campfire at night, without fail someone will praise God for the change he made in Pastor Leatherman."

Many times John gave the same testimony, giving thanks that Jesus had saved him from wanting to be in charge, from anger and from reliance upon his education. He testified, "No longer do I strive and pray that I become holy; 'I have been crucified with Christ; it is no longer I who live, but Christ who lives in me.' " Seeing this kind of life in John caused many to remember what he had taught. And so they often quote him.

Many brothers and sisters could tell other revival stories. One sister learned not to dwell overmuch on these remarkable experiences. She prayed, "Lord, thank you for all you did; now come to us afresh for today's needs."

**Helpers in revival**

For East Africa 1942 was a year of special blessing. Not only did God awaken the Mennonites and other churches; he also prepared messengers to strengthen the revived ones. That was the year in which William Nagenda and some classmates left the seminary a few weeks before graduation. They had been under censure for holding prayer and testimony meetings, and they were protesting the appointment of a theological liberal to the teaching staff. In this way God freed William for evangelistic ministries wherever the Spirit might lead. That was also the year when Festo Kivengere was converted. Festo, who had been a teacher and a supervisor of schools, had for some months resisted the Spirit. One Saturday a younger sister pleaded with him to repent. Later that day Festo made his decision to follow Jesus. William's first ministry to Mennonite missionaries was in 1948, followed by stateside contacts also. In later visits he was teamed with Festo.

# THE BEGINNINGS

Note: Captions appear in sequence; photos were arranged as they fit together.

1 Dhows leaving Mwanza with helpers, baggage and supplies; missionaries also aboard Musoma—Shirati.
2 Baggage and supplies were moved to station by oxcart.
3–4 Timber and sand were transported by workmen.
5 First worship service at the campsite.
6 The first missionary dwelling; Elizabeth Stauffer in doorway.
7 Mennonites are singers and lovers of the Word (by Heidi Wenger).

▲1

▼4

▲3

▼5

▼6

1 The sons of Kisare, 1–r;
  Nathanael (dispenser), Simeon
  (facilitator) and Zedekia
  (teacher); also Martha Simeon
  and child and Susana Zedekia.
2 Zephania and Rusabella Migire
  and their oldest children.
3 Elizabeth Stauffer gave out
  picture cards.
4 Youth who studied at Shirati in
  1940s, some from Kenya.
5 Two Kamageta churches were
  begun before the missionaries
  arrived; at left is Ibrahimu
  Ogwal.
6 The 1941 spiritual life conference at Shirati.

▲ 4

▼ 2

▲ 5

▲ 8

▲ 1

7 ▲

1 Emil Sywulka, a revivalist, helped Elam Stauffer choose Shirati and Mugango locations.
2 Ray Wenger, a beloved bishop, and his firstborn, Daniel.
3 Wenger and Ezekiel Muganda shared oversight of churches.
4 Ezekiel Muganda and Metusela Chagu, enthusiastic revival preachers.
5 Bugufi revival team: Erisa Rwabuhungu, Frederick Bategereza, Gabriel Rwandini and Yohana Baishumike.
6 Stefano & Muse Tingayi, the first Bumangi believers to avoid compromise with pagan marriage customs.
7 Chief Chabwasi, who released land for the Bumangi station, appreciated visits by the Christians.
8 Henry Garber, pastor sponsor of student Daniel Mtoka, visited TMC in 1967 and called on Daniel's father.

67

◀ 1

▼

▲ 3

◀ 4

▼ 5

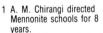

1 A. M. Chirangi directed
  Mennonite schools for 8
  years.
2 Many of the schools had been
  started under a tree.
3 The youth of Tanzania are
  eager for educational opportunities.
4 The growing enrollment of girls
  led to the 1958 opening of
  Morembe School.
5 Musoma Alliance Secondary
  School was also established in
  1958.
6 President Nyerere receiving
  from Joseph Ojiu the MASS
  contribution to assist crippled
  children.
7 Recognizing teachers as the
  foundational element in education, Pastor Masese, like
  others, was diligent in pastoral
  care.

▼ 7

▲ 2

▲2

3▶

◀4

▲6

◀5

1 Lois Eshleman, one of the
  handcraft teachers.
2 In 1952 Miriam Wenger taught
  homemaking at Mugango.
3 Rebeka Mutemwa, matron of
  Mugango Girls' Home 1939–
  59.
4 A course in home and
  childcare skills was begun in
  1964 at Bukiroba.
5 For 30 years Daniel Opanga
  was the church's printer.
6 Nathan Waiga, second
  manager of Musoma
  Bookshop.

▲ 4

▲ 3

▲ 6

▲ 7

▲ 5

▼ 1

1 Nathanael Gomba dispensing
  medicines from the timber
  shed, 1934.
2 Rael Boke, one of the first
  nurse aides.
3 Nyarero Dispensary buildings,
  1952.
4 In ten years Dr. Mack trained
  this team of helpers.
5–6 Dr. Merle Eshleman supervised expansion of Shirati
  Hospital 1951–54.
7 Dr. Richard Weaver, second
  surgeon, was supported by an
  energetic team.
8 Staff nurses on duty: the
  medicine cart, the beds, etc.
  were made by Sam Troyer.

8 ▶

1 Zedekia M. Kisare    Jan. 15, 1967
2 Hezekia N. Sarya    Feb. 18, 1979

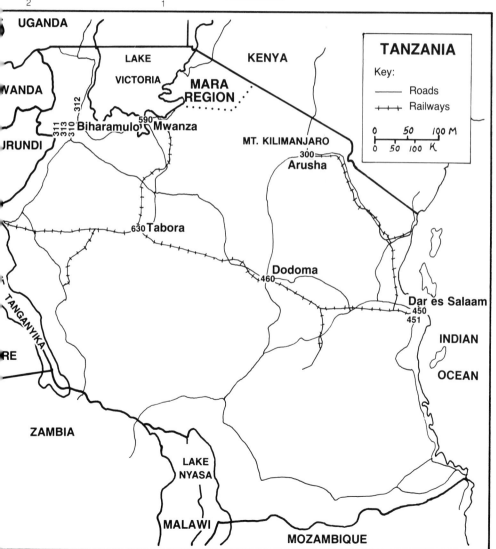

**TANZANIA**

Key:
— Roads
+++ Railways

UGANDA

LAKE VICTORIA

KENYA

MARA REGION

WANDA

JRUNDI

Biharamulo

Mwanza

MT. KILIMANJARO

Arusha

Tabora

Dodoma

Dar es Salaam

TANGANYIKA

RE

INDIAN OCEAN

ZAMBIA

LAKE NYASA

MALAWI

MOZAMBIQUE

71

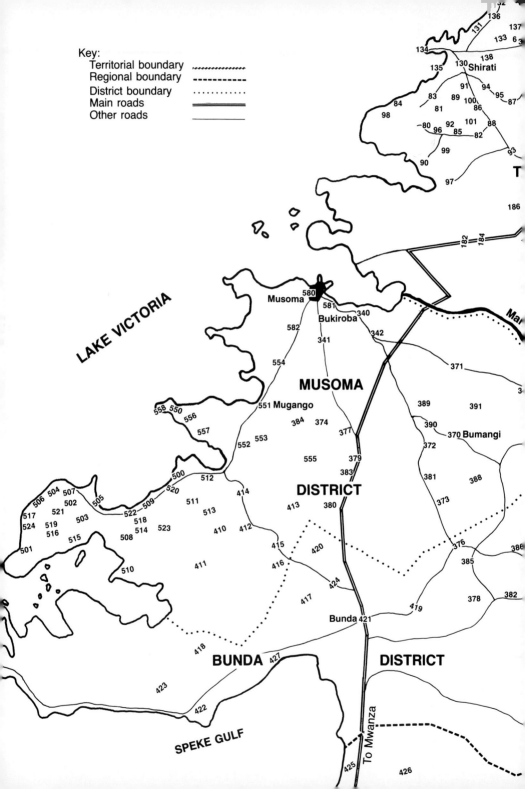

Key:
Territorial boundary
Regional boundary
District boundary
Main roads
Other roads

LAKE VICTORIA

Shirati

186

182 184

131 136 137
133 63
134 130 138
135

84 83 89 91 94 95 87
98 81 100 86
80 92 85 82 88
96 101
99 93
90 97

T

Mar

Musoma 580
581 340
Bukiroba 342
582 341

554 371

MUSOMA

551 Mugango 389 391
558 550 556 384 374 390 370 Bumangi
557 377 372
552 553
555 379 381 388
383 373
DISTRICT 376

500 512
504 507 520 511 414 413 380
506 502 505 509 386
517 521 522 518 513 410 412 415 420 385
524 519 503 523 508 514 416 424 382
516 515 411 417 419 378
501 510 418

Bunda 421

BUNDA 427 DISTRICT

423 422

SPEKE GULF

To Mwanza
425 426

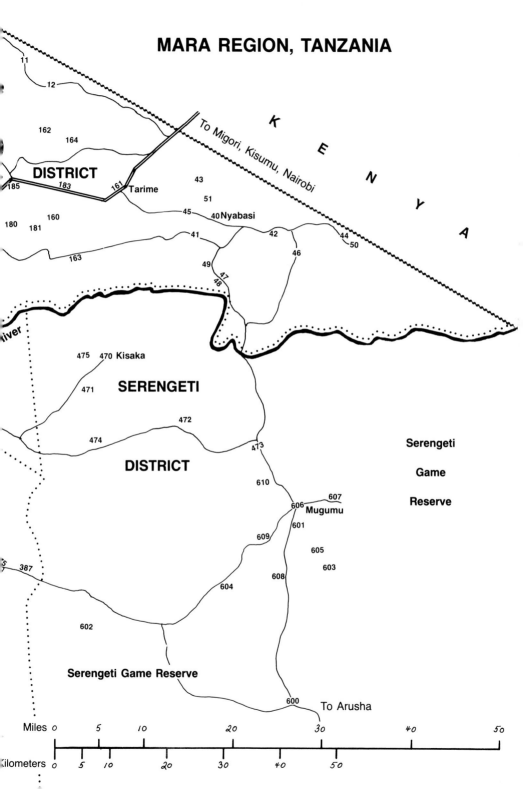

1 The students in leadership training school 1937.
2 One of their examination days.
3 From 1947 onward the Bible school had its classroom.
4 A drum called students to class.
5 The 1956 graduates and teachers.
6 Students in theological college 1967–69.
7 1983 seminar for N. Mara programmed Bible study group (TEE).

▼ 1

▲ 3

▼ 7 ▲ 4

▲ 2

▼ 6 ▼ 5 ▲ 8

1 Bishop counsellors to Stauffer, Amos Horst (center), J. Paul Graybill.

2 Nyambok and Kisare called as pastors 1950, following ordination of Muganda and Mabeba.

3 In 1956 Orie Miller nudged TMC Executive towards autonomy.

4 The August 1960 session of General Church Council adopted the TMC constitution.

5 Kisare and Muganda visited stateside churches 1961.

6 Meso and Sarya visited James & Mattie Harris 1964.

7 Kisare was ordained bishop in 1967.

8 1979 ordination of Bishop Sarya.

▼ 3

2 ▶

◀ 5

▼ 1

4 ▶

1 Majita District Council comprised of congregational delegates.
2 Dar es Salaam District Council.
3 1973 TMC Conference: the ordained, district delegates and heads of church ministries.
4 Naomi Smoker, TMC office secretary 1949–69.
5 Koreni Togoro served 1961 to the present.

◄5

▲8

◄6

◄3   ▲1

▲7

◄4

1 H. Sarya inviting baptismal class to express their repentance, faith.
2 Assisting him with the baptisms are P. Chai, J. Shenk, M. Adongo.
3 A Sunday school class at Shirati.
4 Youth leaders share experiences, plan together.
5 Youth share the gospel thro songs they write.
6 Teams provided medical help to distant churches.
7 Phebe Yoder helped spearhead adult education nationwide.
8 Bishop Sarya supported Bishop Kisare during the funeral of his wife Susana.

77

# PASTORS

1 Nashon K. Nyambok    Dec. 10, 1950
2 Yeremia M. Kabury    Jan. 24, 1960
3 Aristarko M. Masese    Nov. 20, 1960
4 Daudi W. Mahemba    June 18, 1961
5 Daniel M. Sigira    Oct. 31, 1965
6 Dishon M. Ngoya    Nov. 7, 1965
7 Elisha N. Meso    June 19, 1966
8 Nashon N. Nyambalya    June 26, 1966
9 Naftali M. Birai    Sept. 8, 1969
10 Salmon S. Buteng'e    Sept. 15, 1969
11 Manaen N. Wadugu    Oct. 20, 1969
12 Ebanda K. Marukwa    June 20, 1976
13 Phinehas Nyang'oro    July 11, 1976
14 Erasto M. Nyamusika    May 1979
15 Gershon Nyarusanda    June 10, 1979
16 Julius Bulemo    Feb. 22, 1981
17 Eliasafu M. Igira    ″
18 S. Majinge Karuguru    ″
19 Daniel I. Mtoka    ″
20 Sospeter M. Muttani    ″
21 Salmon Nyamugundu    ″

22   23   24   25   26

22 Nathanael W. Tingayi   "
23 Japhet Maiga     "
24 J. Wera Magangira  Mar. 15, 1981
25 Gershon A. Mbudi   Feb. 13, 1983
26 Lawrence S. Makonyu  "

## DEACONS

1   2   3   4   5

6   7   8   9

1 Paulo C. Chemere  Sept. 18, 1955
2 Zephania Koja Migire Dec. 18, 1955
3 Yusufu W. Mwita   Dec. 2, 1956
4 Narkiso Odhiambo  Aug. 27, 1972
5 Eliya M. Wandiba  June 20, 1976
6 Isaya A. Onyango  Oct. 14, 1979
7 Naaman K. Kujerwa  Aug. 29, 1982
8 Eliya M. Magoro   "
9 Naftali M. Mugenyi   "
10 Mishael M. Nyasonga Mar. 6, 1983
11 Fares Sasumwa    "
12 Petro Masanja   Mar. 20, 1983

10   11   12

79

1 W. Ray Wenger
1910–1945
2 Elizabeth Stauffer
1900–1947
3 Nathanael Nyamare
1908–1958
4 Esther F. Troyer
1913–1961
5 John E. Leatherman
1909–1969
6 Alta Shenk
1912–1969
7 Lillie S. Kaufman
1899–1971
8 Martha Jane Lutz
1931–1971
9 Martha Mohler
1939–1973
10 Ezekiel K. Muganda
1910–1974
11 Noah K. Mack
1911–1974
12 Naftali N. Chacha
c1933–1975
13 Frederick Brenneman
1903–1977
14 Nora Snavely
1910–1977
15 Elam W. Stauffer
1899–1981

16 Phebe Yoder
1903–1981
17 Andrea M. Mabeba
1916–1981
18 Edna S. Hurst
1913–1982
19 J. Eby Leaman
1912–1983
20 Susana A. Kisare
1919–1983
21 Misraim Nyagwegwe
1922–1983
22 Raheri Muganda
c1917–1983

# 5.

# GROWTH AND EXPANSION, 1942-50

## Witness in Majita and Kenya

Out of the joy of a fresh experience with Jesus, of newness of life, some young men of Mugango began seeking those who were still lost. Gideon Muga, Dishon Magunira, and others went to Majita, preaching day and night. Because they neglected the care of their bodies, Satan took advantage. For a time Gideon lost proper use of his mind, and four others on the station were also troubled by spirits. Phebe Yoder called together a small group who prayed with them each morning and evening. The four found early deliverance, but for Gideon healing came more slowly.

From Shirati Nikanor Dhaje and Wilson Ogwada witnessed for twenty-two days in Kenya. As their testimonies and preaching penetrated hearts, some men resisted with physical violence. Nikanor was struck on the face, and his lip bled profusely. Later he testified: "But we, because of the fire of God within, were not intimidated and felt no anger against him. Jesus was more precious to us than life itself." This testimony was one of the foundations of the Mennonite Church in Kenya.

At some places revived persons experience persecution. Worldly neighbors penalized them for misdeeds they had confessed. People who loved darkness annoyed and resisted the believers, hoping that they would renounce Jesus, for their confessions and testimonies brought deep conviction.

The missionaries, too, were helped in new ways. Rhoda Wenger testified: "I took satisfaction in the fact that I had not committed any of the gross sins. But then the Spirit showed me my lack of love, backbiting, and jealousy." Dorothy Smoker learned to accept the cross of not insisting on her own way. She gave up seeking the mere praise of people.

As a result of revival in his congregations, Bishop Ray Wenger changed the content of his preaching; for example, he emphasized God's judgment upon sin. He had been trying to build up in Christ those who had been baptized. Through revival he came to realize that many of them had not yet met Christ.

The penetrating light of the gospel caused many to withdraw from the church. On every station the membership dropped. Because of the gross sins some church elders had to confess, they were asked to discontinue preaching; one was asked to leave Bible school for a time. Those who found healing in Jesus were quickly recognized and given their responsibilities again. Some of these persons continue as pillars of the church in 1983, and others have passed on to be with the Lord.

During this time of pruning and nurture, communion services were postponed in all the churches. At Shirati the service not held in August 1942 was rescheduled for April 1943. On that day twelve were baptized, persons who had experienced the joy of newness of life.

## Hunger for spiritual growth

Missionaries and elders shared the burden that the revival continue. Remembering how they had prayed for revival, the brothers and sisters at Shirati established a monthly day of prayer. Many more experienced revival in the annual conferences which met at Mugango in 1943. In the missionary conference William and Virginia Steere led the Bible studies while Metusela Chagu preached in the spiritual life conference which followed. He appealed to God's people to leave the wilderness and to enter the promised land, to give up the controls to their lives so that the Spirit could work through them. Many were helped to take the next step in spiritual growth, and others met the Lord the first time. In September 1944 Brother Metusela returned for a preaching circuit to every station, meetings which many remember with gratitude.

In the joy of personal release and of deep fellowship in the church, the missionaries suggested to the mission board that they send only missionaries who could appreciate revival, who had accepted the way of the cross in their own lives. The board was happy that the missionaries were united in responding to the Spirit, but feared that perchance they were tending toward withdrawal from conference to start a new church. They realized, too, that as a board they were not able to evaluate persons on the basis of the specified criteria. In addition, they wanted time for the missionaries, and the board itself, to be further taught by the Spirit in how to walk in newness of life in brotherhood. So they replied that they would defer sending missionaries for a time. By this time, however, the missionaries had repented of their lack of faith and withdrawn their suggestion. Within a year additional missionaries were on the way.

In 1945 John and Catharine Leatherman and Phebe Yoder went to America on furlough. Their penetrating personal testimonies brought varying responses. Some folks were turned off. Others with hungry hearts noted the joy reflected in their faces; they fellowshiped with the missionaries and found spiritual growth.

Back in Tanganyika, however, revival fires gradually burned low. Looking back, some brothers confessed that they had slacked in obedience to God and in resisting Satan. They put it this way: "We dozed and slept." An additional dimension of need developed, an influx of new missionaries—eight arrived in 1945-46—who had only secondhand knowledge about the revival of 1942. But within they were hungry.

**A fresh wave of revival**

Some of the older missionaries experienced fresh awakenings. In 1946 Simeon and Edna Hurst went to Uganda on vacation, and were helped to a simple walk with Jesus—a walk of prompt repentance for daily sins, and of openness to brothers and sisters, giving testimony and receiving challenge. On their next vacation George and Dorothy Smoker went to Rwanda, where they were similarly helped. Sensing that walking with Jesus in repentance and fellowship was the key to ongoing revival, Elam Stauffer, with the counsel of others, invited a revival team from Bugufi, western Tanganyika. These congregations, Anglican, were known for their joy and testimony.

In November 1946 a team of four arrived: Erisa Rwabuhungu, Frederick Bategereza, Gabriel Rwandini and Yohana Baishumike. A three-day meeting was planned for each station. Because many were praying for a fresh revival, the four were received with great joy at each place. Besides, the guest speakers were seen to be gentle persons with open faces, full of joy and peace from the Lord.

The team went first to Bukiroba. In the first session each brother gave his personal testimony, telling how he had been lost and how the grace of God had followed him. One had stolen some government tools. With much trepidation he returned them, knowing he might receive severe punishment. The Lord touched the officer, who freely forgave him. Another had difficulties in living peacefully with his wife; when he was willing to humble himself and help her with what were regarded as women's chores, he found that their marriage was like new. Another had difficulty in relating to a fellow church leader. But as soon as he confessed his need, grace prevailed. Their testimonies of confession and joy touched many.

On the second day their messages focused on sin, particularly on God's judgments, again illustrated with personal testimony. The next forenoon they held forth Jesus as Savior. For the afternoon, they announced a testimony meeting in which those who found new help could praise our Lord.

After songs and prayer, the station carpenter walked forward, placed a box on the pulpit, and showed the tools he had stolen while he worked in a government shop. As soon as he said that he would return them to the district commissioner, the congregation burst into praise, "Glory, glory, Jesus saves me."[1] Another confessed that he had wished his wife to die because they were not getting along well. His confession touched another who, before the session closed, had also confessed and was released. Each time someone made a clear commitment, the congregation responded with another verse of the glory song. After dismissal, songs and testimonies could be heard across the station; many were praising, and additional persons found release.

Each night Erisa, Frederick, Gabriel, and Yohana met with the station leaders, men and women, for mutual encouragement and to pray for the meetings. In the final meeting, they emphasized how important it is for leaders to maintain close spiritual fellowship, and described the twice-weekly fellowship meetings in their congregations. First they walked together "in the light"[2], that is, they shared the victories and defeats they had experienced. Next they read from the Scriptures and shared fresh insights that came to them. Then they prayed for each other.

Instead of planning a spiritual life conference for 1947, the Mennonites invited Frederick Bategereza and Brother Nyonyintono for a ministry as the Lord might lead. During June and July the two brothers visited each station, bringing public messages and counseling with the fellowship groups. One brother wrote to his prayer helpers, "God's people have been tasting the joys of heaven, though they still live in this world of darkness and strife."

### Joined together in Jesus

In the weeks that followed, our Lord continued to break down the barriers between missionaries and nationals, binding them together in the Spirit. Realizing that they had the same kinds of temptations, they began to help one another to the Savior. Feelings of tribalism were melting away. By origins, there were three groups in the church: Nilotic Luos, the Ruri and Jita peoples, and the Zanaki and Kurya, plus lesser tribes within these larger groupings. But those who loved the Lord rejoiced

84

that, as new persons, they were one tribe in Jesus.

Together they grew in finding God's will, learning to discuss matters until they came to unanimity. Where they could not come to agreement, each was ready to accept the other with his differing views. At times the unity was tested; issues arose which brought rifts within the church. But each matter was resolved in due time because the leaders stood together. For example, Ezekiel Muganda and Zedekia Kisare, knowing each other's commitment to Jesus, could face their disagreements, repent quickly, and find the way together. As another example, John Leatherman and George Smoker, though they were very different in temperament, worked happily on the same station for twenty years—because they were open with each other on the issues that could have divided them.

### Diligence in evangelism

The revival produced real enthusiasm in evangelism. From 1934 until 1942, 15 new churches had been opened; from 1942-50, another 24 were added.

In 1943 Elder Zephania Migire was traveling to one of the outchurches by bicycle; suddenly he realized that he had run over a cobra. In his excitement he fell. Although he could not see the snake again, he saw blood. Believing he had been bitten, he wrote a farewell note to his family and the church. However, after resting for a time he realized that he had not been bitten, climbed onto his bicycle and proceeded. As soon as he arrived at the church, a sister testified how glad she was to see him, recounting how in a dream she had seen what he went through. The whole congregation joined in prayers of thanksgiving for the reminder that Satan cannot hinder the preaching of the gospel. Just before this Zephania had preached against the wearing of spirit fetishes.

### Prepared for service ministries

By purifying his church and bringing the leaders into close fellowship, our Lord prepared the Mennonites for enlarged medical and educational ministries. And long before he had also been preparing persons who would serve. For example, he had led Phebe Yoder to prepare as a teacher and then as a nurse. He guided Noah Mack and Merle Eshleman to prepare for ministries of healing in East Africa. However, when these brothers began to speak of their vision, other missionaries were quick to object, fearing that big hospitals and educational institutions would weaken the church.

So there were many discussions. The development of the medical program was discussed in committee in 1942 and 1943 and in the mission business meeting of 1944. It was agreed to open a dispensary at Mugango, and to begin training for medical dressers at Shirati. The following month, however, the government raised some serious questions and concerns. In response the Medical Committee met twice. Reassured that God had called them to a ministry to the sick, they agreed to develop a hospital at Shirati and to operate a dispensary at Nyabasi; Mugango would be closed for the time being.

As a result, the training of nurse aides was begun in October 1945. A year later at Shirati, Clinton Ferster began to build a maternity ward and a new facility to serve outpatients. The mission board also took a hand in the planning and called for a master plan for development of the medical program.

In 1948 there was an outbreak of smallpox in Tarime District. So that the disease should not reach epidemic proportions with many fatalities, the government undertook to vaccinate half the population. Dr. Noah Mack accepted leadership of the vaccination team; the government provided helpers, nationals with some training and experience, and covered all costs. Within ten days this team had vaccinated 66,000 persons.[3]

For several years the mission had also been discussing expansion of the educational program; higher grades had been added for a few people. Nudged by the persistent request of the church, Phebe Yoder and the Education Committee sensed that the time had come to take further steps. After discussing the matter with the Bugufi revival team, they approached the Anglican educationalists, Lionel Bakewell and Charles Maling, about the possibility of receiving two CMS teachers on secondment.

Within six weeks, in January 1947, two teachers arrived. Isaka Leutetilwa began upgrading Mugango Primary School, adding to the curriculum the subjects needed to prepare students for government examinations at the end of grade four. From among the pupils a school captain and class leaders were chosen. They were responsible to oversee the cleaning of the school compound each morning, for checking personal hygiene, and for leading the morning march. With drums throbbing, reinforced with flutes and such other instruments as local ingenuity could provide, pupils entered enthusiastically into the march.

James Mwigilwa similarly began preparing the Shirati school for government registration. At the same time, Mennonites Samuel Ngoga and Mikael Muganda were sent to Katoke, Teacher Training Center, Bukoba, to be trained under a dean among teachers, the late Capt. J. T. Bennett.

### Finding guidance together

Following these encouraging developments, a special meeting was called, a joint session of General Church Council and the missionary legislative body, to review developments and to adopt a policy. They met at Bukiroba on February 20. In the worship period, many testified that the Buguf team had helped them grow in their walk with the Lord. They gave thanks for converted teachers, like several brothers in the Buguf team, teacher-evangelists in the governmental system. This perspective helped the missionaries turn over to the Lord their fear that persons with higher education would leave the mission. They also chose to identify with African aspirations. Recognizing that parents and elders should decide how to provide schools for their children, the missionaries committed themselves to work with them, whether within or outside the national structures.

The meeting came to unanimous agreement to operate accredited schools within the governmental system and to receive grants-in-aid to make this possible. Prayer was offered for funds to assist in the training of teachers. Several elders were chosen to serve with the missionaries on the Education Committee. Thanking God for his leading, the meeting adjourned.

When board secretary Orie Miller arrived on his biennial visit, the missionaries enlarged on their report of the steps taken, and invited some free-will offerings to assist the church in opening primary schools. On Miller's recommendation, the mission board affirmed the program as undertaken. Several contributions got the program underway, but soon funds were provided through normal budgeting processes.

The year 1947 witnessed another educational initiative. Shortly after the opening of the first accredited primary school, Hilltop School was started at Bukiroba for the children of missionaries. It offered an English-language curriculum geared to American patterns so that children could transfer into other schools during furlough years. Teacher Grace Metzler capably taught both academic subjects and Bible.

The Lord continued to revive his people, enlarging the circles of fellowship. Brothers and sisters in Bukoba, Ngara, Musoma, and Mwanza found opportunities to encourage and strengthen one another. Anglicans, Lutherans, Mennonites, and some from Africa Inland

Mission came together in occasional conventions; they made fraternal visits in each other's congregations. Thus they were prepared to work together in education. Those who had teachers shared with those who lacked; spaces in post-primary schools were shared from church to church. CMS supervisor, Frederick Bategereza, used his free time to visit and encourage God's people in the several geographic areas he served.

Such fellowship and sharing enabled the Mennonites to participate in the central government's Ten-Year-Plan, 1947-1956, for educational expansion. The national goal was to provide four years of elementary education to half the school-age children and to increase the proportion completing grades 8 and 12. In local government planning sessions, Elam Stauffer and Phebe Yoder projected—by faith—that in Musoma District the Mennonites would open three schools each two years and in Tarime District a school a year.

As they moved ahead, the Education Committee experienced that opening schools involved more hard work than they had assumed. Their first priority was pastoral care for the teachers—their spiritual and temporal needs—and to help them teach Bible lessons in a meaningful way. At this time the committee became aware of some of the larger issues. How can the churches contribute to the developing public educational system so that the schools benefit both pupils and community? How can more middle and secondary schools be provided, since many pupils were completing grade four with no further schooling available to them?

**Interchurch cooperation**
Because all the churches were facing these questions, the education secretaries of Church Missionary Society, Church of Sweden Mission, Africa Inland Mission, and Mennonite Mission met in Mwanza in February 1950 to discuss these very issues. Interestingly, the delegates were hosted by Marie Sywulka, who continued in a ministry of prayer and counseling for many years after the passing of her husband in 1945.

The delegates recommended to their respective missions the establishment of a forum to handle educational issues of mutual concern. The missions ratified the proposal and established Lake Missions Education Council (LMEC). A year later Swedish Free Mission also joined.

Recognizing that they could better provide for their church constituencies by pooling their resources, LMEC members agreed that each mission undertake to build and administer one post-primary school and that each such school be managed as an alliance by the churches sending pupils. CMS would expand Katoke to be the teacher training college for

LMEC missions. Proposals were drafted for the Lutherans to establish a secondary school west of the lake and for the Mennonites to build another on the east; AIM would build a vocational school.[4]

In a second meeting, several delegates drafted plans for *Bible Studies,* a series of study guides for each elementary grade. The Mennonites and AIM picked up the project; Dorothy Smoker, Florence Tilley, Catharine Leatherman, and Matt Nyagwaswa wrote the manuals.

For the Mennonites the main educational project in 1950 was building their first boarding school for boys, grades 5-8. Because the funds provided by government covered only the cost of concrete and timber, it involved a lot of volunteer labor. Each of the five church councils was assigned to build one particular building. Following a staggered schedule, they went to Bumangi, teams of youth and elders. Traveling on foot, they carried food supplies, cooking pots, and some tools. However, the teams from North Mara were accommodated by lorry. Each group sang as they traveled, building group spirit and praising the Savior. Work began at sunrise and, with a meal break, continued until sunset. They dug foundations, collected stones, and made bricks; then they erected the building and thatched it. Everyone worked together, out of love for Jesus and the desire that youth have opportunity for an education.

### Growth of national leadership

While the missionaries were busy in evangelism, and in expanding the medical and literature ministries, God was preparing the church elders for leadership responsibilities. Quite unexpectedly he took to himself Bishop Ray Wenger, in what seemed an untimely death. Ray and Miriam had been involved with AIMers in preparation of a Jita hymnbook, selecting songs and checking translation. With a fever which did not respond to the usual medication, Ray was taken to Musoma Hospital. Within two days, on June 9, 1945, he went to be with the Lord. The next day a large crowd gathered on Mugango station for the funeral and heard the Word proclaimed by Elam Stauffer. His body was laid to rest in a grave now marked with a simple headstone and large frangipani bushes.

One of Ray's last testimonies was, "(Jesus) must increase, but I must decrease." Dedicated to our Lord, he was diligent in evangelism and in counseling and praying with people. Even today a teacher pays tribute to Ray for punishing him as a child; Ray had found him engaging in improper behavior. Ray had good fellowship with the Christian community, and the family appreciated this level of interest in their child. The larger community, too, even the Asians and Europeans, knew him to be a man of God.

With no advance warning, leadership responsibilities had fallen upon the church elders, and God enabled them for their tasks. One month later new missionaries, Levi and Mary Hurst, succeeded Ray and Miriam at Mugango. The elders had a large part in training Levi and Mary, setting the pace for a new pattern, the missionary as a helper and resource person, not in charge.

The missionaries took to heart the matter of preparing national leadership. In January 1946, six months after Bishop Wenger's death, Elam Stauffer led General Church Council in putting into writing the emerging polity of the church. From past minutes he had summarized decisions made by the council, bringing them together under appropriate heads. The group reviewed each issue, point by point. Either the earlier decision was affirmed, or amendments were made, or the matter was deferred for further study. Two days were insufficient for such intensive review, so the group met again in April.

Two years after Ray's death, God gave another reminder that one's earthly tenure is uncertain. Elizabeth Stauffer had suffered heart trouble in 1943, but was restored and able to go about her work, particularly her prayer ministry. During their 1947 vacation trip to Kampala she died and was buried near to the missionary heroes Hannington and Mackay and Apolo.

The preparation of leaders continued apace. In January 1947 Leatherman and Stauffer reopened the Bible school. The new curriculum included more biblical studies, since enrollees were expected to have at least four grades of education. But only twelve started the course, and a few of them soon dropped out. Musoma shops were beginning to stock fine clothes, transistor radios, and bicycles. So there was a scramble for good-paying jobs. The bright lights attracted youth to the big towns. The conversion of old military lorries to passenger buses facilitated their travel. While the Bible school now had its own attractive classroom building, some potential leaders responded to lesser goals.

### The literature ministry

Musoma Press began operations in December 1946, preparing catechism cards and other items needed by the congregations. The first books to be printed were the Jita primer, *Father and Mother,* and the Zanaki hymnbook, *Hymns of Praise to God.* The *Messenger of Christ,* then in its seventh year of publication, was enlarged and printed as a small magazine. Its warm evangelical message attracted serious readers, and it began to circulate throughout East Africa.

Since their mimeographed songbooks were tattered and congregations were growing, Ezekiel Muganda, Rhoda Wenger, and George Smoker were asked to prepare a new songbook in Swahili. After they had agreed on the hymns to be added, Rhoda obtained permissions to use copyrighted numbers. She translated a few not then available in Swahili, such as "Jesus Paid It All," and grouped the hymns under appropriate headings. *Spiritual Songs* was released in 1950, an edition of 5,000.[5]

Having a press hastened the preparation of the church's own catechism. Theologian John Leatherman prepared excellent questions and answers, making it very useful to evangelists and catechism teachers. Elam Stauffer produced a companion volume to prepare catechumens for their baptismal vows and church responsibilities.

**Efforts for expansion**

Remembering the home board's desire to open new fields beyond East Lake, the missionaries were diligent in searching out possibilities. They were eager to move beyond Musoma District. In 1940, shortly after the opening of Nyabasi, they investigated possibilities in Kondoa-Irangi, a 1,400-mile trip. The colonial government refused the application without explanation. The following year, hearing that all German missionaries had been interned for the duration of the war, Elam Stauffer and Merle Eshleman undertook a trip to Bukoba to offer help to the orphaned mission. But as soon as they reached Musoma, they learned that those stations had already been committed to other missions. At another time they checked out the possibility of going to Biharamulo. Then they learned that during the war government would not grant rights to land. After the war, colonial officials discovered that EMBMC was not included in the commonwealth list of recognized mission societies. Again the door to expansion was temporarily closed. The mission board undertook to qualify for such registration.

In the late 1940s, the missionaries developed a burden for the 100,000 people in Mbulu who had only two missions among them. As soon as Eastern Mennonite Board was duly recognized, John Leatherman and others made three safaris to check out possibilities in the Mbulu area. They were welcomed by the local Lutheran missionaries, and the Mbulu chief marked out a plot; only confirmation from central government was still needed. The church invited John and Catharine Leatherman and Daniel and Susana Sigira to open that station.

While waiting for final approval, John and Catharine camped in the area, learning the Mbulu language. Shortly the Lutheran mission board objected that their local missionaries did not have authority to welcome a new mission. Besides, they had not known that some missionaries displaced in China were scheduled to come to Mbulu. Leatherman was greatly surprised by these developments, but he chose not to claim any rights. He suggested that, since a dispensary and school had been promised to the local populace, the tribal elders should choose whether the Mennonites or the Lutherans should open the new station. They chose the mission with which they had some acquaintance. John and Catharine departed, pondering deeply why God had sent them to wrestle with a difficult language and why, as soon as they had begun to make some progress, they were asked to leave. While they had no answers, they rested in the faithful God whom they served.[6]

# 6.

# RECOGNITION OF LEADERSHIP, 1950-60

### Finding the Mugango pastors

Brainstorming, prayers, and discussions had come to fruition in a conviction shared by church elders and missionaries—the time had come to install national pastors. General Church Council had come to agreement on goal and procedures: in 1950 two pastors should be installed at Shirati and two in Mugango-Majita; the districts should be prepared through special meetings for biblical instruction and united prayer; selection should be made by the churches to be served, with each member eligible to make nomination; only church elders were eligible to be nominated; evidence of God's leading would be the unanimous nomination of two pastors.

Bishop Stauffer prepared a series of teachings with four themes: (1) unity of the Spirit in the church, (2) personal sanctification of life, (3) every believer is a priest of God, and (4) qualifications and characteristics of the pastor. The two-day meetings were to be times of mutual upbuilding, including teaching, testimony and admonition, open discussion and united prayer. In March and April he conducted the first series at Shirati, at Mugango, and at Butata, with a second series in May and June.

Because many brothers and sisters of Mugango-Majita had entered wholeheartedly into the work, looking to God and avoiding human scheming, Stauffer called them to meet August 21-23 at Butata for teaching on the qualifications and characteristics of a pastor. He invited pastors and elders from the other districts to participate in leadership of the meetings.

The grace of God hovered over the crowded Butata church as open hearts received the teachings, expecting God to lead. The pastors and elders were unanimous in sensing that the time had come to receive names. Bishop Stauffer called the congregation to special prayer, everyone kneeling.

Then he invited members to bring their nominations to his tent where he would be waiting with the team of pastors and visiting elders. He encouraged the congregation to give themselves to spontaneous singing and prayer during this time.

An older member came, nominating two brothers. The next person presented one name. Sixty-five persons responded one after another, men and women. Nearly everyone named the same brother; many of them also nominated a second, and a third was named once only. The sister who made this nomination was called privately and given opportunity to tell how she found guidance. She answered, "Since I live at a distance and our evangelist is the only leader I know, I brought his name." When she learned that only she had named him, she withdrew her nomination in favor of the names presented by others. (Five years later, he was ordained.)

Ezekiel and Raheri Muganda were called to the tent and informed that Ezekiel had been named. He replied that he had indeed heard the call of God; therefore, they were ready to respond to the call of their church. Andrea and Rebeka Mabeba also witnessed to a call and readiness to take up the work as God would direct.

With happy faces the team of leaders returned to the church. Bishop Stauffer gave a testimony of praise, announcing the names of Ezekiel and Andrea. Immediately the whole congregation was on its feet, singing "Glory, hallelujah, praise to the Lamb," all seven verses. Several shared testimonies; others led prayers of thanksgiving, and the meeting was closed. However, the hymns and testimonies continued outside the church and also in the paths as people fanned out walking to their homes. A group of women went to the kitchen to prepare food for the guests from a distance, singing as they worked.

During this time the elders and pastors began planning an ordination service. Though they realized that persons would come from all the station areas, they decided to make this service a part of a spiritual life convention already scheduled to be held at Nyamuribwa. When they discussed how to divide responsibility between the pastors, one elder urged: "Let us build upon the unity God has given us; let's not move them. Let the Mjita Kaneja continue serving among the Ruri people and the Ruri Mabeba among the Jita."

People from all the stations gathered at Nyamuribwa in a large shelter built of sisal poles and covered with branches and sorghum stalks. For three days they fed upon the Word of God and praised Jesus in testimony. The climax of the meeting was the ordination of Ezekiel and Andrea on Sunday, October 8, 1950. By the laying on of hands and by prayer, they were commissioned to preach the gospel and shepherd the churches. Again hymns spilled over one another.

## God also led at Shirati

In October Stauffer and a few pastors went to Shirati for the final teachings there. When members were ready to present nominations, many came, and six elders were named, four of them only once each. As agreed, the bishop did not announce the names; he appealed, "Let us continue in prayer, and meet again next month. Secondly, should anyone realize that he brought a nomination out of self-will, he may come to me or write a letter." Before he returned to his station the next morning, two had come, each withdrawing a name.

Stauffer returned in November, and during these meetings another brother privately removed his nomination. One fringe name remained; Stauffer spoke to the nominator and he, too, withdrew it.

Two nominations stood, elders who had been named by the majority. Zedekia and Susana Kisare were asked privately whether they could accept this call to the pastorate. Zedekia responded, "I have long been aware of God's call; I am ready to take up the work." Nashon and Dorka Nyambok similarly witnessed to a call and to their availability.

When the names were announced, with one heart the people sang, "Glory, hallelujah." In their deep joy, some laughed and others wept. Everyone was shaking hands; some were dancing in praise to God. One after another the believers greeted Zedekia and Nashon and wished them God's blessing. Vivian Eby, who had been their teacher, promised to pray for them. James and Ruth Shank, who had been leaders of the pastoral team, received them "with both hands." They looked forward to serving together for a limited time, knowing that after a few years they would retire from the field.

Zedekia and Nashon were ordained on December 10, 1950, in a special service in the Shirati church.

## New efforts in evangelism

The warmth of church unity and the joy of finding national pastors fueled new efforts in evangelism. The number of catechumens increased and many were baptized. Whereas from 1943-50 three churches had been opened each year, from 1951-60 seven churches were opened every two years. A few stories will give an idea of the scope and intensity of evangelistic efforts.

The leading evangelist in the Shirati area was Zephania Migire. Although only three churches—Tatwe, Busurwa, and Mikondo—list him as one of the pioneers, in many instances he shared in the initial contacts in a community, but left the follow-up to others. In some cases, as in Kenya, he continued helping evangelists who were starting new churches. Each Friday afternoon after he had finished teaching, he would travel to location. On Saturdays he and the local leader visited from house to house and then led an afternoon service. On Sundays he would preach again and return home. Through the years Zephania shared in establishing twelve churches. Even while he attended a training course for new deacons at Mugango, he spent weekends assisting in evangelism among the Luos of Nyang'ombe, Majita.

Shirati Hospital staff members also helped, only a few of whom can be named. Dr. Merle Eshleman assisted Migire at a number of locations. Each Sunday Ezekiel Kachare went to some preaching point. Elma Hershberger went out with her tent, sometimes for a few days and sometimes for a week, helping the leaders of emerging churches. She liked to involve younger missionaries in her trips so that they would experience the joy of learning to know people in their own homes.

At Nyabasi, each Friday was devoted to evangelism around the station. A group met in the Hurst home for a bit of tea and prayers, and then fanned out to visit neighbors. Each Sunday a number of the brothers went to their respective preaching points. The Nyabasi Christians also reached out to the people of Bwiregi, traditional enemies of their own clans. In 1948 Alexander Makoreri and Eliseba Makena moved to Kangaliani; in 1950 Yeremia and Esta Kaburi left Nyakunguru and moved to Mangucha. These new churches had grown out of evangelistic safaris by Noah and Muriel Mack and Simeon and Edna Hurst.

Throughout the Musoma district the brethren were also diligent in evangelism. From 1951-60 many churches were opened, especially in Mugango-Majita and Bumangi areas. And God blessed the evangelists with fruit. Today, many of these older leaders have opportunity to relate to their spiritual grandchildren. For example, one of the 1983 leaders at Tegeruka is a grandchild in faith to Hezekiah Sarya who moved there in 1948.

From the beginning the evangelists and catechists were occasionally brought to the station for a week of spiritual refreshment and retooling. Musa Adongo, evangelist at Masinono, offered to host the 1952 Mugango-Majita seminar in his church. For two weeks he and his people looked after the needs of twenty evangelists and their teachers, George and Dorothy Smoker, and Mahlon Hess. These men learned from each other, particularly from the older men like Paulo Chemere, Samson Marore, Paulo Musyangi, Daudi Osoya, and Naftali Mugenyi. In preaching the gospel they had moved from place to place. They had weathered many difficulties: shortage of funds, inadequate clothing, and sometimes lack of food. To attend spiritual life conferences they sometimes traveled on foot for three days, carrying clothing, bedding, and food supplies. In recalling these experiences they praised God afresh for the way he had provided for them.

The elders met monthly for fellowship, mutual admonition, and business. On one occasion Ezekiel Muganda praised God for sustaining them in the years of pioneering, experiences that the next generation could hardly appreciate. To make his point, he described the building of a house. In a foundation several courses of stones are hidden beneath the ground level; they are never seen again, yet they carry the weight of the whole house. The brethren responded with "Glory, hallelujah," dedicating themselves to continue in their hidden ministries.

On the weekend near to full moon, students in the Bible school were taken on evangelistic safaris. Their efforts were instrumental in opening doors in Ikoma and in Kisaka. In 1954 they made one trip with their fellow student, Wilson Ogwada, to his community in Kenya.

### Ikoma, Kisaka, Tarime, Musoma

The first Mennonites to search out the hunter people of Ikoma, ninety miles southeast of Musoma, were Clyde Shenk and Daudi Kirangi (whose home was there) in 1948. The Bible school team provided follow-up until Daudi and Dorka Mahemba moved to Robanda in 1950, and then continued helping them from time to time. After a year the first class was baptized: Samuel Bwanana and wife, Paulo Kisaka and wife, and Petro Makondo, a diligent messenger in the chief's court. Through the hard work of George Smoker, Robanda Primary School was opened in 1956. Salmon and Lois Buteng'e joined the worker team in 1959, with Salmon teaching carpentry. This team also evangelized among the farmer peoples who were migrating from Kenya and clearing the virgin soil in nearby Mugumu. The population increased, a town developed and a hospital was needed, a hospital that would finally be built in 1980.

It was in 1938 that Clyde Shenk first evangelized in Ngoreme, forty miles northeast of Bumangi, among Bantu peoples most of whom had not yet heard of Jesus. In 1946 the missionaries resolved to build a new station, either in Kisaka or in Kenya. The people of Ngoreme were placed in the monthly prayer calendar, and the Bible school team made occasional visits. During this period some Luos from Kenya moved into the Kisaka community. When they asked for an evangelist to live among them, Zedekia Kisare responded and with Susana served there 1949-50. After he was transferred, Joash Lore and Daudi Kirangi shared leadership responsibilities. In 1954 Nyiboko Primary School was begun, and Clyde and Alta Shenk were placed at Kisaka to open a station.

Because more Mennonites were moving into the towns, pastors and elders began to sense their responsibility to provide pastoral care, and to see the large opportunities for evangelism. Nashon and Dorka Nyambok were chosen to go to Tarime; they moved in 1953, and a fine church building was erected. Ezekiel and Raheri Muganda were called to Musoma. At first the pastor traveled the eighteen miles by bicycle from Mugango; in 1954 they moved to Musoma. The church building was dedicated in November 1955.

God blessed this large team of evangelists, using their upright lives, their helpfulness to neighbors, and their preaching. There was also diligent teaching of the Bible in schools, as will be noted later. These ministries produced good growth in membership: from 1935-42 an average of 25 per year; 1943-50 an average of 40; 1951-60 an average of 178.

**More primary schools**

In 1953 the Mennonites had to face up to a difficult question. To fulfill the projections made by Stauffer and Yoder in 1947, they would need to build 17 additional schools by 1956. Since only eight schools had been built in the five years past, the question was whether 17 could be built in the next three years, or whether these opportunities should be given to other agencies. Because the missionaries had already experienced how much hard work is involved in opening schools, they would have preferred to undertake only a portion of the openings. However, recognizing that such an important decision should be made by African church and community leaders, they resolved to help the national church give leadership in its communities; they would help build as many schools as General Church Council would undertake to manage.

To begin their discussion, the council listed the communities which had requested a school, a total of 19. Government grants-in-aid were available for 17 schools, so they chose as many communities, dividing them appropriately between the church districts. In this bold planning, they were not intimidated by the hard work which lay ahead. Their desire was that the children have opportunity to go to school—their own children and their neighbors'.

Each district council was made responsible to report to the communities whose requests they had submitted—size of plot needed for a school, community responsibility for two classrooms and two teachers' houses, and duties of the parents' committee. Since the elders were expected to supervise the project until it was completed, they would need to assess whether the community could organize enough voluntary labor to carry through. When all contacts were completed, they would confirm to the education secretary which communities they believed were a good risk.

Although education secretary Hess was pleased to take these requests to the government authorities, he had fears that these bold proposals might not be accepted; perhaps he was recommending some communities which might not be able to complete satisfactory buildings. After some discussion, the North Mara Education Committee gave permission for schools to be built under Mennonite management in seven new communities. Requests from other churches and agencies were likewise approved. The committee felt satisfied that the total package made for a good distribution of schools throughout the district. Likewise the committee in Musoma adopted a district plan which included 10 new schools under Mennonite management.

The education secretary then got busy recruiting potential teachers and finding places for them in training colleges. Since all LMEC churches were opening new schools, he could not get enough places at Katoke. But two colleges in older communities were able to help. He also arranged for the Lutherans and Anglicans to second more teachers. Occasionally he was called into the districts to help work out problems that arose, such as suitability of plot, location of buildings, and recruitment of pupils. The church leaders gave themselves wholeheartedly to this expansion effort, working side by side with community people. In places where local people lost their enthusiasm, it was the church people who saw the project through to completion.

### Boarding schools

During this same period, two boarding schools for boys were being built, one at Bumangi and another at Shirati. Primary education had been extended from six to eight years. In rural areas grades 5-8, called middle school, needed to be offered with boarding facilities. Knowing that the youth of this age-group are making decisions which determine the direction of their lives, and believing that church and community leaders would emerge from these schools, churches in North America contributed funds which made possible permanent buildings. The Bumangi unit replaced the district school, opening in 1954; Shirati was a totally new school and opened in 1955.

Middle schools offered academic training along with practical handcrafts and agriculture. The care of livestock involved a seven-day, twelve-month schedule. The teachers also lived at the schools, reinforcing their teaching by example. Among the teachers whose personal and family lives were a good influence were George Bihondwa, Phinehas Nyang'oro, James Lifa, Nathanael Tingayi, and Sospater Muttani.

In 1954, five primary schools were also opened, in the following year there were two, and then in 1956, 10. Church elders and missionaries were full of praise to God; they had reached their goal.

The Mennonites now had a school in each area where they had adherents, 11 schools in Tarime District and 16 in Musoma District, one third of the schools in these districts. Through their hard work, together with that of the Roman Catholics, and of the native authorities, central government had reached its goal: half the children of the nation now had opportunity for primary schooling. But in East Lake, with its late start, only 36 percent were in school.

New goals were set for the period beginning 1957—goals to improve the quality of the primary schools and to provide more middle and secondary schools. The Mennonites were given funding for two boarding schools, one for girls in grades 5-8 and one for boys in grades 9-12. Ivan Sell and Allen Byler had major roles in building these schools.

Morembe Girls' School, opened in 1958 with Rhoda Wenger as headmistress, reflected the growing enrollment of girls. The excellent training given in the girls' homes on the several stations helped overcome opposition to education for girls. The personal efforts of *Mama Elimu* (The Lady Who Promoted Education), Mary Hancock, added momentum to this change. Like a number of her predecessor civil servants—administrators, doctors—her life and work strengthened the hands of the missionaries.

The boys' school, Musoma Alliance Secondary School, was formally opened in 1959 under headmaster John S. Shellard. (The first class had been recruited in 1958 and accommodated at Alliance, Dodoma.) From this school the church began recruiting some of its teachers and medical personnel, looking forward to the day when some of these persons would become church leaders and pastors.

The pupils for Morembe and Alliance came from the primary schools. From their teachers they had learned to like school. Many had learned to take God seriously; moral values had been formed. Teachers who taught the Bible with the same enthusiasm as the three R's had made deep impressions. Many teachers also preached in the Sunday worship; in the recently opened schools, the service was held in one of the classrooms.

Of the dedicated teachers who are well remembered for their Christian testimony, only a few can be named: Elisha Ruzika, Caleb Randa, Jonathan Ndayanse, Beldina Yusufu, Herman Kataraia, Arphaxad Maiga, Martin Ephraim, James and Esther Olimo, Phillip Lwegayula, Erasto Mugendi, Wilson Saidi; others not known to the writer came after them.

The government of Tanganyika laid particular emphasis on moral and character training, inviting each of the faiths to provide religious instruction to their adherents in the school timetable. All churches provided daily Bible instruction in the schools they managed. Beginning in 1948 teams of missionaries and local Christians made weekly visits to government schools near to them; in a double period they taught Bible lessons and/or the catechism. For a number of years, Rhoda Wenger gave leadership to the Bible teaching in Mennonite schools, also helping the Mennonite volunteer teachers. When she was asked to oversee Morembe, she shed some tears about leaving what she considered had been one of her greatest ministries.

Through their schools, the churches made a significant contribution to the emerging new nation. As in other developing nations, many of the leaders in Tanganyika—leaders in education, in business, in civil service, in politics—have been persons of character from Christian schools. With the churches having managed two thirds of the schools, that was a contribution of considerable magnitude. The churches also made a broad contribution to the emerging public educational system. Church leaders provided the initiative for starting schools and in locating them. Dedicated teachers set a good tone and high standards. Church educationists like Solomon Eliufoo, Sidney Clague-Smith, Joel Ngeiyamu, Allen Gottneib, Stanford Shauri, and Donald Jacobs helped shape the system and develop curricula with the needs of the new nation in mind.

Occasionally church leaders thought ahead to the time when the government would undertake its responsibility to provide educational opportunities to the total population. Anticipating that the first step would be taking over the management of all existing schools, they felt great satisfaction that the church had had a major share in laying the foundations for the emerging system of public schools. As they looked forward to the time when they would be released from day-to-day management of schools, they envisioned the church focusing its efforts on more Bible teaching in all schools and on pioneering new forms of educational effort—for example, providing for the crippled and retarded.

Mission leaders also recognized another responsibility. In 1959 from the Mennonite schools alone, 1,000 pupils completed grade 4, 120 grade 8, and 40 grade 10. From all the schools in Musoma and Tarime Districts, there were three times as many. With the limited opportunities for further schooling, it was clear that unless these youth had access to appropriate literature, many would revert to illiteracy. The Mennonites made two responses. With the help of Phebe Yoder, church leaders opened schools at Kwikerege and Shirati for youth who could not continue in the grant-aided systems. Secondly, Musoma Bookshop was opened in 1960, with Grace Stauffer as manager assisted by Nathan Waiga.

**Expansion of medical ministries**

During the period 1950-60 God granted much larger opportunities for ministries to the sick. Dr. Merle Eshleman, affectionately called *Obimbo,* The Big One, was greatly appreciated for his ministries to women and children. He had trained a good team of practical nurses including Rael Boke, Dorka Atieno, Esta Ngoga, Eliseba Yakobo, Ludia Achola, Eleazar Ogendi, James Nyakyema, and Joshua Abuya, just to name a few. This team helped many sick persons, and bore a good witness for Jesus.

Recognizing that many Shirati patients needed help he could not give, Dr. Eshleman requested the recruitment of a surgeon and the provision of appropriate facilities. He requested early arrival of the surgeon so that he himself could oversee the building program. The mission board recruited Lester and Lois Eshleman, a surgeon-anesthetist team. They also provided a mechanic-plumber, Sam Troyer, and two youth volunteers, Hershey Leaman and Chris Peifer. These men laid a pipeline to bring water from the lake, constructed beds for the two wards, and built equipment for the X-ray and surgery. Soon the skillful ministries of surgeon *Orembe,* The Swift One, were widely known, and people came from distant points to be treated at Shirati.

Persons afflicted with Hansen's disease, leprosy, came to the hospital in increasing numbers. Beginning in 1948 Obimbo had treated two persons with the new medicines then available. After two years the patients were able to return home. As a result more persons came for

102

treatment; unfortunately, however, they did not realize the importance of continuing with treatment after they began to feel better. Someone was needed to provide continuing oversight to the emerging leprosy program. Nurse Elsie Cressman, who arrived in 1954, found that 200 persons had enrolled and begun medication, whereas only 90 came to the clinic on treatment days. When Shirati leprosarium was opened on March 2, 1954, seventy persons from 13 tribes came for treatment.

People from a distance were given opportunity to build a house and to have a small garden within the leprosarium, a sizable plot on the lake-shore. Some enterprising persons equipped themselves with a canoe and net to provide fish for their own tables and to get spending money. After three years there were 400 persons under treatment; 300 of these lived with their families in the unit.

By 1960 a total of 1,000 had been treated, and hundreds of them were in complete remission; because many went home without being checked out, one can only estimate the number. Many had been helped spiritually; 70 had been baptized.

The health ministries from Shirati began to benefit other stations from 1957 onward. Nurse Velma Eshleman was sent to Kisaka to open a dispensary. Under her oversight, small dispensaries were also opened at Bumangi, Mugango, and Bukiroba. She visited each dispensary monthly, while one of the doctors checked them out at least once a year.

### From fatigue to praise

The end of his first missionary term left Dr. Lester Eshleman fatigued with hospital problems, at loggerheads with the revival fellow-ship—though he recognized that the Spirit was indeed working throughout East Africa—and frustrated with African culture. His reactions to these experiences separated him from missionaries and African Christians who could have helped him. The spontaneous revival song, "Glory, hallelujah, Jesus is cleansing me," irritated him. Brothers and sisters sang it when they met; in their fellowships it rang out again and again—in praise for blessings, and whenever someone took another step of surrender to Jesus—an outburst of joy and release which goaded Lester's imprisoned spirit. Consequently, as their 1957 furlough approached, he concluded that he would never return to Tanzania.

However, the God of grace followed him. God led him to a medical practice in rural Pennsylvania not far from his boyhood home. Slowly his mental energies were restored and his spirit refreshed. God blessed his ministry, and he became known as "the doctor with a shepherd's heart."

The frequent letters of invitation to return to Shirati, and the refreshing of the Holy Spirit during a two-year furlough, enabled Lester and Lois to resolve, "We will go back to Shirati and identify deeply with those committed Christians; we will join in the revival song."

As they neared Shirati, a long line of jubilant people waited by the road to receive them. Reaching the doctor's residence at nightfall, the group encircled the house with joined hands, singing a joyous welcome. Just then the sound of the generator was heard and the lights came on—symbolic of the brother relationship which was to follow.

Lester continued to grow through fellowship and mutual help in the revival group. Freed from fear, he could share his struggles and find release. When conflicts arose he was able to discuss matters and find the way. During the whisperings and confrontations that developed as independence approached, one ardent politician was heard to complain, "We cannot drive any wedge of separation between him and his African colleagues." Twenty-eight years after that commitment, Lester and Lois are still praising our Lord. They are having an extensive ministry at Kilimanjaro Christian Medical Center, one of Tanzania's consultant hospitals, including regular visits to Shirati.[1]

### Discipling one another

The Spirit continued to move in vigorous revival from 1950-60. Fellowship groups met regularly on each station, in some of the other churches, and in the government middle school, Musoma, during the tenure of Headmaster Emmanuel Kibira. Leaders from the revival groups met monthly at Bukiroba to strengthen and admonish one another. Brothers and sisters freely visited one another, in their homes and in their churches.

For the Mennonite spiritual life conference of 1956, William and Sala Nagenda and Festo Kivengere were invited as speakers. Attendance overflowed the shelter built in the center of Bukiroba station. Many persons found help. As customary, the Mennonite hunters brought a number of game animals to provide meat to garnish the ugali, rice, and vegetables served to conference guests.

Each issue of *Messenger of Christ* reflected the blessings of the Lord. The Mennonites were happy to read testimonies from brothers and sisters in many parts of East Africa and to report what God was doing in Musoma. From time to time Muganda, Leatherman, Kisare, and Stauffer were invited to preach in Mwanza, in Bukoba, in Maseno, and in Mombasa. And their families were blessed through the guests who came to them. The Muganda children learned to anticipate the arrival of the weekly steamers—what sort of guest might come this time? Ezekiel was very hospitable, eager to learn from others.

Revival fellowship was seen at its best in connection with weddings and funerals. For example, during 1958 the brothers and sisters welcomed Salmon Sarige Buteng'e's request for help in finding a suitable mate. They counseled with him, with a suitable young woman, and both families; Lois Mangwe accepted their counsel and his proposal. Because Sarige had been deprived of his rightful share of family resources, the fellowship helped bring together a gift to Lois's family. (She had grown up in Mugango Girls' Home, and the usual bride price was not called for.) In the wedding service they shared in the preaching and prayers. They provided a wedding feast and made it the occasion for Christian testimony.

Whenever the Lord is at work, Satan is also busy, sometimes imitating. There were persons who sang the revival song, used the revival greetings, and attended fellowship meetings, but their real interest was material progress.

Satan also made special efforts to trip up the missionaries. All of them were in favor of revival, for it made their work easier. Revived persons readily accepted their guidance. Even when nationals needed to challenge a missionary on something, they came in humility. When there was good attendance in fellowship meetings, missionaries were tempted to take credit. Some saw themselves as better than others. Some tried to guide and promote revival in the energy of the flesh rather than in dependence on the Spirit. In all these matters, God was faithful and helped them to repent.

## Steps toward national independence

The anticipation of independence emerged gradually. Soldiers who served overseas during World War I heard about aspirations and plans for independence, for example, in India. While as children they had thought of white people as gods, the Africans now became convinced that whites are no better than others. In the training camps they had experienced the vices and sins of whites; on the fronts they saw them kill one another. The war itself was an exercise in the use of force to attain national goals. Having observed other cultures, Africans began to sense the values of their own, to feel good about their traditions and customs. Such Africans began to look down on white people; there was a growing unwillingness to be governed by them.

In the cooperatives farmers had gotten a taste of being able to control their own affairs. They received more profit for the cotton they sold. Soon each local co-op erected a small headquarters building. Area groupings bought existing ginneries from the Asian entrepreneurs and built some new ones. The regional headquarters established central offices and a small hotel. In time they built a plant and produced their own textiles. They were gaining good experience in working together, helping to shape their own future.

In 1954 Julius Nyerere, a secondary school teacher, began to urge that the time for independence had come; he organized Tanganyika African National Union (TANU). In time he resigned from teaching and traveled throughout the country, sharing his vision in every tribal center and town. The colonial government, and missionaries too, had doubts and some fear. All of them professed the goal that Tanganyika become a self-governing nation, but all emphasized that the people were not yet ready. The local people, however, were happy for a way to express their aspirations. Christians who were careful as to how far they entered into politics were criticized by the radical fringe as trying to put themselves in a good light with white people. With its democratic goals, TANU continued to grow and, in the first elections, overwhelmingly defeated the multiracial party and a fringe party.

Nyerere's meeting with his own tribe, the Zanakis, was the last in his swing through the nation. He said, "Every British colonial officer knows that independence is near and that his basic task is to train Tanganyikans. They are working at it, but we citizens are not yet ready!" He urged families to follow better health practices—more light and ventilation in houses, and a clean water supply. He was most urgent in his appeals against drunkenness and bribery. The tribal elders nodded to each other, affirming what he had said and murmuring some distrust of the younger politicians.

Whenever Nyerere discussed independence with colonial officials, he appealed to the United Nations guidelines which specifically stated that the trusteeship should obtain until the populace asked for independence. His negotiations were successful; by 1960 Tanganyika had attained internal self-government. Julius Nyerere was the prime minister.

**Foundations for church autonomy**

Preparations of the church for self-government dates back to the beginning, the special efforts to prepare women to be responsible partners in Christian homes and congregations. Each station had a weekly meeting in which women learned sewing and the Scriptures. Elma Hershberger, assisted by missionary wives, gave leadership at Shirati. On several occasions spiritual life conferences geared to the needs of women were held. The homes for girls—one on each station—had a formative ministry in the lives of hundreds. The girls largely supported themselves from their gardens. They attended the station schools and had additional Bible and music classes, plus evening devotions, led by the missionary-in-charge.

The Mugango home, under Miriam Wenger and Rebeka Mtemwa, developed to enrollments of forty. In 1952 Miriam offered the first course in homemaking: Bible, cooking, sewing, child care, and home management, using only local resources. Many of the alumnae of the girls' homes are now the wives of church leaders. Several of these men affectionately call Miriam their "mother-in-law."

The calling of nationals to leadership was another important step in preparation of the church. Elam Stauffer had given leadership to 21 ordinations (19 persons) from 1950-61.

In 1955 the church began calling deacons, that is, servant counselors who also looked after physical needs, following the model of the apostles (Acts 6). In September 1956 the churches of Mugango-Majita called Paulo Chemere, Hezekia Sarya, Aristarko Masese, and Daniel Sigira. In December the Shirati churches called Zephania Migire, Isaya Obiero, and Dishon Ngoya.

In January 1956 Bumangi called Jona Mirari as pastor and Elisha Meso as deacon. In the following December Nyabasi called Nathanael Rhobi Nyamare as pastor and Yusufu Wambura Mwita as deacon. Like the first four pastors, these men also were given some special training—at Mugango in 1958. Nyamare, however, did not complete the course; on June 10 the Lord took him to himself.

"The winds of independence" occasioned a new method of choosing persons for ordination. To find guidance through prayer and intense spiritual fellowship requires time, self-denial, and submitting one to another. It was easy to bypass these disciplines when the country was straining toward independence. When it had become clear that additional leadership persons were needed, there was general agreement to find another way to move ahead. General Church Council resolved that persons who receive three fourths of the votes cast may be ordained.

The Nyabasi church called Yeremia Marara as pastor and Naftali Nyangi as deacon early in 1960. Near the end of the year, Mugango-Majita called Musa Adongo as deacon and Hezekia Sarya and Aristarko

Masese, former deacons, to be pastors. Daudi Mahemba was called to the pastorate in Ikoma in June 1961. Each main segment of the church now had national leaders.

### "Partners in obedience"

During his 1956 visit Secretary Orie Miller took Bishops Elam Stauffer and Simeon Hurst with him to visit the leadership clusters of the Lutheran Church of Northern Tanganyika, Moshi; the Anglican Diocese of Central Tanganyika, Dodoma; and interdenominational Africa Inland Mission, Shinyanga. At each place they discussed the prospect of autonomy for the given national church and learned what steps had been taken in preparation. Then Miller met with the Executive Committee of Tanganyika Mennonite Church (TMC)—by this time the name had been agreed upon—and nudged them to begin preparations to carry full responsibility for all that is essential to the life of the church.

When he came again in 1958, Miller read Philippians 1:5, explaining that some missions had committed themselves to prepare their counterpart churches for autonomy, and to dissolution of the local mission apparatus. The goal was "partners in obedience" (quoting a theme from the International Missionary Council's 1957 meeting). For TMC the next step would be to work together, so the church could learn to know all the ministries they would carry. He directed that for one year the executive committees of the mission and the church should meet together, each committee handling its own agenda with the other sharing in discussion.

Several persons were chosen to draft a constitution for the church. With a reminder about the basic principles of Mennonite faith, they were directed to prepare a constitution that would speak to the issues with which TMC must grapple.

The year 1959 marked the 25th anniversary of the founding of the TMC. To observe the occasion, an official deputation made a visit: Paul Kraybill, new secretary of the board, together with his mentor, Orie Miller; Ira J. Buckwalter, treasurer; and John R. Mumaw from Eastern Mennonite College, former teacher of many of the missionaries. These guests were hosted on each station, and they addressed anniversary meetings for area outchurches.

Given opportunity to read the first draft of the proposed constitution, the deputation members affirmed it as suitable to the Tanganyika church, and undertook to present it to the Lancaster bishops.

Early in 1960, with seventy-five nationals teaching in the church's schools, it was agreed that the first positions to be nationalized should be the educational leaders. When the Education Committee met to choose persons for these positions, they could not come to agreement. Several persons made this a matter of special prayer, and when the committee met again the following month, they quickly chose Phinehas Nyang'oro as education secretary and Josiah Muganda as education assistant; for a time they were to work with and learn from their predecessors, Mahlon Hess and Laura Kurtz. Accepting the heavy responsibilities laid on them, these two brothers served well.

About this time the first national was appointed as station superintendent. Daniel Mato Sigira had oversight of Mugango for a time; later he was transferred to Kisaka.

The church elders also were readied for additional responsibilities. Longtime service in a variety of situations provided invaluable preparation for many. During some brainstorming on patterns appropriate for the autonomous church, George Smoker told Elam Stauffer, "You built better than you realized." Smoker affirmed the value of the pattern established in 1938: members choose elders to handle congregational matters; the elders meet in a district council to handle matters of common concern; the district council chooses delegates to the General Church Council, the ultimate authority. The whole council agreed that the same pattern should continue for the days ahead and that the functioning councils simply be given new names suitable to an autonomous church.

# 7.

# STEPS IN AUTONOMY, 1960-66

### TMC recognized as self-governing

TMC's draft constitution occasioned some tense soul-searching discussions by the Lancaster bishops and the mission board. There were those who wanted to make rigid restrictions on fellowship with Christians of other denominations, on separation from the world, and on non-participation in the military. The mission board and bishops met again on July 5, 1960, to prepare a response. After more prayer and debate, Ira Buckwalter spoke up: "What I saw in that church was the work of the Holy Spirit; let us harbor no attitude, take no step, that will hinder him." The bishops came to a landmark decision: That since Tanganyika Mennonite Church and Lancaster Conference share equally in the grace of Jesus, Lancaster will not presume to determine the positions of TMC, but will share concerns and suggestions. A deputation of three had been chosen to go to Tanganyika for fellowship, presenting the concerns of the bishops and to pray with TMC leaders for guidance of the Spirit.

Amos Horst, Donald Lauver, and Paul Kraybill represented the two boards in special sessions of the General Church Council held at Shirati. Early in the meeting one brother identified a special concern of some delegates, that the national church actually be given some authority; specifically, that Phinehas Nyang'oro, education secretary designate, should promptly assume full responsibility and not go on as a helper. After some discussion a resolution was prepared and supported.

The council spent some time on the articles of faith, particularly the relation of church and state, and heard the concerns of the Lancaster bishops. After discussion on ordination and on TMC relations with Lancaster Conference, the draft constitution was adopted. Everyone joined in the revival song. That was on August 25.

"Now you are a church responsible for your own life," said board secretary Paul Kraybill. "In the days ahead we will bury the mission. Plan together the ministries you will want to carry forward, and estimate the financial help you might need. Place the missionaries in the roles you have for them. Register Tanganyika Mennonite Church with your government, and then we will turn over to you the rights of occupancy to station plots, the buildings, and the motor vehicles. We will assist you with some finance, if you do your part."

Immediately the delegates spontaneously moved to the chairman's table, placing coins and notes in a thank offering to God. TMC had attained autonomy without having had to struggle for it. In further discussion, it was agreed that self-government become effective on October 2, 1960, and that each congregation have an appropriate celebration on that day, concluding with a special offering for the central evangelism fund. In the election of officers, the delegates showed their appreciation for their missionaries by choosing John Leatherman to continue as secretary. As treasurer, they chose Elisha Meso. As bishop, Elam Stauffer continued in the chairman's role.

### Fraternal visit to America

To broaden the vision of Tanganyika Mennonite Church, the mission board made it possible for Ezekiel Muganda and Zedekia Kisare to visit the churches of North America from June through August 1961. The visit would also bless brothers and sisters in America, many of whom were eager to meet leaders of this church for which they had prayed for many years.

Kisare and Muganda preached in churches of all the districts of Lancaster Conference, and in others as far away as Indiana and Ontario. They brought greetings and preached in sessions of Virginia Conference, Mennonite General Conference and Lancaster Conference. They visited Eastern Mennonite College, Goshen College, Mennonite Board of Missions, Mennonite Publishing House, and other points of interest. They were hosted in several voluntary service households, learning to know Christian youth who had given themselves to serve the church for two-year periods.

In every place they were received with eagerness and great joy, for they were the first nationals to visit the churches which had sent the missionaries. "The gospel from their lips was very clear," said many. "They touched us where we live." In fact some who had reservations about the missionary enterprise stated openly that they had changed their minds.

Back home again, Kisare and Muganda visited each church district and recounted the blessings they had experienced. As they fellowshiped together, questions about America quickly gave way to another subject.

111

Kisare and Muganda—impressed by the diligent painting and decorating of buildings and towns then underway—knew what was on their minds. In the independence celebrations being planned, to what degree might Christians participate? Some brothers were under pressure to become village leaders—should they accept?

Everyone could affirm the principles of the party, TANU, which were based on the premise of the equality of all men and spelled out in practical duties to neighbor, as from the Scriptures. It was easy to see that the gospel had been a major factor in preparing the nation for independence. Not only had many of the emerging leaders come from Christian schools, but across the country there was also a nucleus of serious Christians. They had experienced freedom from guilt, freedom from overpowering lusts, freedom to put others first—inner freedoms that had made them different, a creative minority in their communities. Church leaders were sensing that if the nation was to grow and mature, it was not enough for Christians to be "light"; they would also have to be "salt," that is, the conscience, of society. Such thoughts gave them pause, but they knew that the living Christ would lead in each issue as it arose.

### National independence

On December 9, 1961, the British flag was hauled down and the new Tanganyikan flag was unfurled. Hand in hand with their national brothers and sisters, the missionaries also celebrated, thanking God for independence without bloodshed. They joined in praying for Prime Minister Julius Kambarage Nyerere and his government.

The joy of the populace could be seen in their smiling faces and in their bearing and vigor as they walked. United in their concern to build a strong nation, they responded to the call of *Mwalimu* (Teacher) Nyerere to wage war on their basic enemies: "ignorance, sickness, and poverty." From time to time Nyerere called on Christians to set the pace in nation building, particularly in self-reliance and national unity. In fact some communities chose a trustworthy Christian to be chairman or treasurer in local government.

Soon after independence *Mwalimu* committed the reins of government to his second in command, Rashidi Kawawa. He climbed into his LandRover again and visited each region, emphasizing to his audiences that progress will come only through hard work and self-reliance; he urged people to work together through their new government. Soon Nyerere was chosen as the first president of the duly constituted Republic of Tanganyika. After the 1964 revolution in Zanzibar, the island and the mainland were united to form the United Republic of Tanzania. Following a mutiny of the army, many persons marched and sent letters to show their support for Nyerere.

On behalf of TMC, Bishop Stauffer sent a telegram to the president expressing support for his goals and pledging prayer support. On hearing this, the late Bishop Stefano Moshi, a Lutheran and then chairman of the Christian Council of Tanzania (CCT), warned the Mennonites that the church dare not align herself with any government, not even a good one. "Every government is temporary," he said, "and the church must always be ready to serve her Lord under whatever government will follow."

### Special training for leaders

To equip them to serve well in a land which had been newly awakened by independence, special training was planned for TMC leaders carrying major responsibilities. Orie Miller had taken the initiative in the establishing of Mennonite Theological College. The Bukiroba station was graced with fine classrooms, dormitories, and a chapel. Students were hand-picked: pastors, teachers, evangelists, and persons who had done well in Bible school. All classes would be taught in English so that students could have access to the many Bible study helps available. The syllabus of the East African Association of Theological Colleges was followed.

The college opened on August 7, 1962, under the leadership of Donald Jacobs and Dorothy Smoker. Other teachers were John Leatherman, George Smoker, Phebe Yoder, Robert Keener, and Paul Waterhouse. Catharine Leatherman taught the women Bible and home-making. Sixteen students enrolled, persons who were under a call and had served the church. They quickly developed close spiritual fellowship, and the church's executive committee learned to draw upon their counsel. The students found Jacobs' theology class, with his anthropological insights particularly helpful. By laying the Scriptures alongside the teachings of African traditional religions, they found larger dimensions of truth, relevant approaches to tribal customs, and sometimes a third way between African and Western cultures. When crucial insights were presented, attention became so intense one could have heard a lizard scamper across the wall. All the courses, geared to prepare workers to deal with the issues facing modern Africa, were appreciated![1]

### Pastoral care of youth

Autonomy in the church and independence for the nation helped

113

Mennonite leaders place greater value on their youth, recognizing that eventually the tasks of the church would fall to them. Shemaya Onyango Magati, chosen as youth leader in 1960, worked hard to channel the energies and enthusiasm of youth into building the church. In 1962 the Tanganyika Mennonite Church Youth League (TMCYL) was organized, with Daniel Imori Mtoka assisting Magati in leadership. Persons up to age forty were counted as youth, so the younger missionaries also joined, among them Daniel Wenger who had been born in Tanganyika and had returned as a youth volunteer.

Each congregation organized a branch of TMCYL, responsible for cleaning the church, receiving offerings, helping in the Sunday school, and bringing messages in song. If a conference was held at their church, they also helped to build a large shelter for a meeting place, to look after guests, and to cook. Youth groups planted gardens, prepared and marketed sisal fiber, and sold their services as ways of covering expenses.

Each year the youth came together in TMCYL annual meeting. There were choir competitions, Bible studies, teaching on subjects such as preparing for a vocation and finding a life companion, and periods for open discussion. Hezekia Sarya, Robert Keener, Clara Landis, and others gave significant help in the early years.

Parents and elders carried a real burden for the youth who had scattered to the larger towns seeking education and jobs. As a first step in pastoral care, Mahlon and Mabel Hess were transferred to the capital city, Dar es Salaam. Arriving in April 1963, they quickly had names of a hundred young Mennos to be searched out and ministered to. The following month they held their first worship service in Arnatoglu Hall; for a few weeks they met in a member's apartment, and then in a classroom of Dar es Salaam Technical College. Within a year the church was granted right of occupancy to a plot adjacent to the college. Hess was also relief and service administrator for CCT, responsible for getting food to famine areas, for finding resources for development projects, and for helping refugees who had come to Tanganyika, some looking for new homes and others for educational opportunities. Because these duties rapidly increased, Daudi Mahemba was assigned to give pastoral care and leadership to the developing Mennonite congregation.

An autonomous church, seeking to enter our Lord's harvest fields, needs workers with a variety of skills. By personal arrangements, Esrom Maryogo, Joram Mbeba, and Bernard Muganda found their way to the United States to study. Then the church began to sponsor students in Mennonite colleges. Harun Maitarya and Julius Mattijo were the first, with Kembo Migire and Josiah Muganda following. Others were sent for vocational training—Sospeter Muttani in carpentry, Paul Ogina in mechanics, and Eliasafu Igira in bookshop management. In 1965 four graduates of the Bukiroba theological course—Shemaya Magati, Daniel Mtoka, Naftali Birai, and Barak Orondo—were chosen for further training in church ministries.

Because of the goodly number of students sponsored in or helped to the United States, the Mennonite Church became known in East Africa as the church which excelled in making overseas training available. These students hoped to serve the church when they returned, and the church leaders also had large expectations. While these expectations were not always fulfilled, one can anticipate that part of this harvest is yet to come.

During the same period Mennonite Central Committee's (MCC) Teachers Abroad Program also brought staff to Tanzania to help in building up a number of secondary schools, teacher training colleges, and a few hospitals.

### The leadership of Jacobs

In 1962 Bishops Stauffer and Hurst called a meeting of the ordained and other delegates to choose a national bishop. Satisfied with the way the church had picked up its responsibilities, they sensed that it was time for them to retire. They were thankful for the way twelve tribes were working in fellowship, bound together by the Spirit of God. Two names emerged from these discussions, but because neither received two thirds of the votes, the matter was deferred. After a year of prayer and consultation, another meeting chose Donald Jacobs to give bishop leadership for a time.

On June 20-21, 1964, the church held a special celebration at Shirati, a send-off for the senior bishops. There were songs, stories, speeches, prayers, farewell gifts, big meals, and much reminiscing. In farewell messages Elam and Simeon praised God for what the years of service had meant to them—a time to grow together with their brothers and sisters. They committed the church to Jesus, her Head.

When Jacobs assumed leadership, people had high expectations, for he was devoted to the Lord and committed to the development of the church. Just as the nation, with large visions and aspirations, announced its development plans, he also proposed some specific goals for the next five years. The Executive Committee adopted these goals, committing themselves to pray and work to increase membership from 5,000 to 12,000, the pastor team from 16 to 36, and congregational leaders from

100 to 200. They also proposed to open churches in four additional towns and urged elders and lay Christians to seek out persons in their communities who had not yet believed.

Another goal was to boost giving in the church. Elam Stauffer had worked hard at this, encouraging tithing, and had suffered some tongue lashings for his effort. Remembering occasions when he had similarly offended and had to repent, Elam's testimony became the occasion for mutual repentance and fresh bonds of love. Africans felt free to tell him that one of the names given to him had been *Obano,* the one who always had an answer. Jacobs built on these foundations of openness, quick repentance, and persistent teaching.

A parallel effort was to strengthen the economic base of the church. Mennonite businessmen in North America provided funds from which Tanzania Mennonites could borrow to start personal business ventures. Seventeen projects were approved and launched, including hammer mills, fishing enterprises, and tractors for custom work. These were largely unsuccessful.

### A surge of church growth

The church was growing and additional pastors were needed. Daniel Sigira and Dishon Ngoya were ordained at the end of 1965, and in June 1966 Elisha Meso and Nashon Nyambalya were chosen and installed.

From 1961-66 TMC grew more than in any previous period. During this period the pastors baptized 600 persons a year. Existing congregations were growing and five new churches were opened each year. Revival and autonomy had injected new dynamic into leaders and laity. The evangelists were reaching out. Bible classes in elementary and secondary schools brought many youth into the church. Jacobs and the pastors struggled to provide nurture to these new Christians.

Beginning in the stormy years leading up to independence, the church also experienced increasing sifting. Some sought material advantage and others a name and position. Some returned to polygamy with its male privilege. Some resorted to occult powers to answer life's dilemmas. The traditional gods seemed more immediate and could be manipulated, while Jesus remained sovereign. In the midst of these pressures, others accepted him as Lord, the center of their existence; in them Jesus broke the power of evil, making their lives a blessing to many.

The Mennonite schools were flourishing, strengthened by the hard work of Amos Mutaragara Chirangi, who succeeded Phinehas Nyang'oro as education secretary. Each year he challenged the teachers with some goal from the Scriptures. Occasionally he called them together for some teaching, for discussion, and for mutual encouragement. He also sought special training opportunities for them. He took steps to improve the schools in every way: examination results, health, handcrafts, and sports. A ready writer, he compiled many reports, leaving files that are a storehouse of information for historians.

Since each of the denominations had experienced an influx of young believers, much more teaching material was needed. The Christian Council of Tanzania prepared a new series of Sunday school lessons, with John and Catharine Leatherman writing a segment. Through the good efforts of congregational leaders and the youth, by 1968 these lessons were being used in most of the TMC congregations. A few persons also enrolled in home Bible study.

During this time of growth and expansion, the church gave more responsibilities to its secretary. Kembo Migire, the first national to serve in this role, gave more structure to the office and records. He spearheaded the calling of nationals into leadership responsibilities, helping to bring TMC into step with the times. As secretary, he had oversight of all church employees; he also served on the Finance Committee. In committees and in informal discussions, his colleagues looked to him for wise counsel.

A newsletter, *The Voice of TMC,* was launched with Gideon Muga as first editor, followed by Eliam Mauma, church secretary, who succeeded Migire when he returned to college. The *Messenger of Christ* continued its release of testimonies and of biblical expositions; it was a major bond among the revival groups of East Africa. *Spiritual Songs* continued with a wide circulation in all denominations.

In 1962 Tanganyika Mennonite Church began to get acquainted with the Mennonites of Ghana, Nigeria, Zaire, Zambia, Rhodesia, Ethiopia, and Somalia. Delegates from these churches met in Limuru for a time of mutual upbuilding, discussing how to live as people of peace in restless Africa—newly independent nations with some conflicting interests, each building up its military. In 1964 Mathieu Kagadi and Elmer Neufeld from Zaire made a fraternal visit to TMC. Later Nashon Nyambok, Eliam Mauma, and Elam and Grace Stauffer visited among the Brethren in Christ of Rhodesia and Zambia. In 1965 in Bulawayo, this cluster of churches formed African Mennonite and Brethren in Christ Fellowship (AMBCF), proposing to meet every four years.

The churches which relate to EMBMC also began to meet each second year for mutual admonition, with a view to undertaking joint

117

evangelism in some new places. The East Africa Area Office, Nairobi, was established to facilitate such relationships, consultation, and joint projects.

### Development of the healing ministries

Shirati Hospital continued to expand its ministries, with Hershey Leaman as administrator.[2] Arrangements were made for the van from African Medical Research to serve church communities which were distant from existing dispensaries. For a time the Mission Aviation Fellowship plane was chartered a week each month to ferry a doctor and helpers to the outlying dispensaries and to clinics at the Masinono and Kenyana churches. When they found a critically ill patient, he was flown immediately to a hospital appropriate to his need.

These ministries were enhanced by Radio Call intercommunication between Shirati, Nyabasi, Kisaka, and Bukiroba. Dispensary staff could call the doctor for guidance on difficult cases, or in an emergency call the plane.

The Flying Doctor Service brought a variety of specialists to Shirati to help patients with special difficulties and for in-service training of staff. Dr. Harold Housman was the link to their involvement; later he joined their staff as an eye doctor and pilot. Shirati came to be known for its research and pioneer projects. Medical schools of East Africa began to incorporate Shirati findings into their teachings.

The Shirati School of Nursing was opened on January 7, 1960, with Alta Weaver as sister tutor and Drs. Lester Eshleman and Harold Housman assisting in teaching. The first class included five young women and eight young men. In 1964 a course in midwifery was added. The goal of the school is to train Christian young people in nursing skills; effort is made to recruit persons who are ready to give themselves to helping those in need.[3]

From the beginning the doctors and nurses at Shirati sought to help people in spirit as well as in body. When the patient load increased, Yohana Waryuba was chosen as hospital chaplain. Fluent in five languages, he was widely known as a counselor. His face glowed as he shared the gospel and many were helped by his visits. Yohana's highest joy was to pray with persons who had made the commitment of faith in Jesus.

# 8.

# EMERGING PRIORITIES, 1966-74

### The first national bishop of TMC

"Let us move beyond our differences; Jesus is our Head," said Ezekiel Muganda after Zedekia Kisare had been chosen the first national bishop of Tanganyika Mennonite Church.

At the beginning of the selection process—in 1962 and 1964— nearly half the delegates had nominated Muganda. While people were praying that God show his will, there was something of a tug-of-war between Bantus and Luos. Earlier there had been occasions when some would have split the church, but always there were a few, like Muganda, who stood in the breach and made peace.

After the first class had graduated from the theological college, Bishop Jacobs again called the church to prayer for selection of a bishop. In February 1966, the pastors met for prayer and discussion, to discover whether there was sufficient unanimity to proceed. A few testimonies laid bare the real issues. On the second ballot, Kisare received nearly all the votes. Muganda accepted this as the will of God.

Bishop Kisare likes to recall that shortly after this, a refrigerator was offered for sale; Muganda, Kisare, and many others wanted it. Quickly Muganda responded with a proverb: " 'Not every man can grow a beard'; let our leader have the refrigerator." In this way he showed his full acceptance of Kisare as bishop. The acceptance was mutual; Bishop Kisare and Vice-Chairman Muganda worked shoulder to shoulder.

In a special prayer meeting on the same day as the selection, Bishop Jacobs committed leadership of the church to Bishop Kisare. The ordination service came a year later, at Bukiroba on January 15, 1967; Donald Lauver preached and Elam Stauffer gave a testimony. Bishop David Thomas, moderator of Lancaster Conference, delivered the ordination charge and offered special prayer for Brother Kisare.

The following day Bishop Kisare began an itinerary, hosting his overseas guests on brief visits to the main church in each of the districts.

At each place there was opportunity for informal fellowship, a message in the church, and a feast for the guests.

Later each district held a formal reception for their new bishop and his wife, Mama Susana, decking them out with garlands of flowers and serenading them with hymns written by the youth for the occasion. There were meditations and speeches, then the presentation of gifts and a big feast. During the celebrations at Shirati, the master of ceremonies wound up his speech with an appeal, "In leadership, use the rod sparingly; be careful not to break the horns of the sheep." Kisare was deeply touched: "By God's help I will never do this. Thank you for such straightforward advice given in love." The audience affirmed this exchange with a vigorous round of applause.

As his first special project, Kisare established Mennonite Center in Musoma, providing guest rooms, a restaurant, and a meeting room to accommodate committees, seminars, and travelers.

Facing the need to call more persons into church vocations, the council of ordained leaders also reckoned with the difficulty of transferring a pastor who has been called by his own district. To avoid that problem, it was agreed that pastors be called by the council itself. They chose Naftali Birai, Salmon Buteng'e, and Manaen Wadugu, who were ordained and installed in 1969. In 1972 Marko Kisigiro was chosen as pastor and Narkiso Odhiambo as deacon.

In this same year the church conference chose a Swahili name for the church, *Kanisa la Mennonite Tanzania* (KMT), the Mennonite Church of Tanzania. They also adopted the third revision of the church polity.

### Responding to the Arusha Declaration

In February 1967 the political party TANU promulgated the Arusha Declaration as a way of hastening national development. This landmark proclamation called on people to work together as was customary in their traditional culture, urging them not to wait for external help but to become self-reliant. The Declaration commended careers in agriculture and craftsmanship and laid the foundation for some specific policies: (a) each person should have only one primary source of income so that available jobs can be spread more widely; (b) basic industries shall be nationalized; and (c) the schools, likewise, shall be nationalized so that they serve the total population.

Since the churches had been managing two thirds of the schools across the nation, the change of management proceeded by stages. Very promptly secondary schools and teacher training colleges were taken over, and in 1970 the primary schools. On October 8 Bishop Kisare and Educational Secretary Chirangi formally turned over the Mennonite schools—37 primary schools and seven others still in developmental stages.

Since the churches had been released from this heavy burden, government therefore appealed to them to redirect their energies into religious instruction in all schools so that moral character would be developed along with the mind and the body. In response CCT developed *Grow in Faith,* a series of manuals for each grade in the primary schools. A. M. Chirangi and Joseph Shenk shared in writing these manuals. For the secondary schools, *Elements in the Christian Life* was prepared by writers from CCT and Tanzania Episcopal Conference.[1]

After the Arusha Declaration the Mennonites expanded their School of Domestic Science; it had grown out of the teachings given in the Bible school and the 1952 course at Mugango. Since the school received applicants regardless of religious background, the course attracted many girls and women. Because of the high caliber of teachings, it was widely acclaimed. The head teachers who served up until 1983 were Phebe Yoder, Miriam Wenger Shenk, Velma Eshleman, Viola Dorsch, Erma Wenger, Margaret Kisare, and Rachel Igira (now in second incumbency). Rhoda Togoro, an assistant, has the longest teaching record. For a period, Rhoda and Stella Newswanger conducted some sewing classes with women in Nyabangi settlement.

Mennonites were also involved in adult education. Phebe Yoder, who in the 1940s had prepared literacy primers in Jita, Kuria, and Zanaki, later shared in preparation of a Swahili primer which came to be used nationwide. Over the course of twenty years she had trained many literacy teachers. Traveling about in her caravan, *Baraka* (Blessing), she and her helpers sold many literacy and religious books in the village settlements. Everywhere she went she carried her stethoscope and some medications. Constantly she was counseling people and praying with them; there were many names on her prayer list.

As regards agriculture, Tanzania Mennonites had been subsistence farmers from childhood. Long before the Arusha Declaration many of them had been participating in the farmers' cooperatives. Some of them had been called to leadership. Eliakim Kuboja gave excellent management to the co-op at Bugoji, Bunda, for twenty years. Wilson Machota developed the Morotonga, Mugumu, co-op on patterns that increased its profitability. In response to the Declaration, TMCYL established an agricultural project at Tarani, beyond Bumangi. Working with the youth were missionary Leroy Petersheim and two volunteers from America, Don Stoltzfus and Ken Brunk. The project developed into a village settlement.

## Kenya, Biharamulo, Mwanza

For twenty years, 1950-70, the Tanzania Mennonites had seen their schools as their chief channel of evangelism. But some began to look beyond their own communities. In 1965 Hellon and Joyce Amolo were sent to Suna, Kenya, as resident evangelists, specific follow-up to thirty years of evangelistic visits from Shirati. The first contact had been in the mid-30s. Some Suna youth had enrolled in Shirati school, living in the boys' dormitory. After the 1942 revival Nikanor Dhaje and Wilson Ogwada had preached in the area, with follow-up by Zephania Migire and Dishon Ngoya. Working with a local leader, Elnathan Orero Anuro, they established several churches. Zedekia Kisare, Wilson Ogwada, and others assisted.

In 1962 Jonathan Mabeche had begun preaching at Mohuru. In 1965 many of the Luos from Ngoreme returned to Kenya. Those led by Naaman Agola went to Songhor and the Elifaz Odundo group went to Kigoto. With churches established in several areas, Clyde and Alta Shenk were sent to give leadership. Although request to establish a station had been refused in 1945, 1954, and 1963, permission was now granted, and the Shenks moved to Migori on May 15, 1968. Clyde and Alta visited each of these clusters to discover how to help them spiritually. They helped the congregations in evangelistic outreach and in building permanent meetinghouses.[2]

Travel helps people to expand their horizons and to think beyond their own groups. Jackson Wera Magangira, a student in the theological college, went to Biharamulo to visit bereaved relatives during a school vacation. The family was participating in a new village settlement, Ichwankima, which did not yet have an evangelical church. Bishop Kisare, sensing an opportunity for church expansion, commissioned Magangira and Ebanda Marukwa to investigate during the next school break. When they returned with the district commissioner's letter of invitation, TMC leaders saw this as confirmation of God's call.

In 1970 the Bible school helped the Magangira and Marukwa families in their move to Ichwankima. Promptly they built houses and planted maize and cotton. In their work and contacts they bore witness to the Lord Jesus. Then Wera was chosen by the village commune to be trained as a dispenser. He undertook this four-year course, but during school breaks he still helped in evangelism. He returned as the settlement's dispenser, but soon was transferred to a dispensary near Tabora, and Ebanda continued alone with the preaching, catechizing, and baptisms at Ichwankima.

The church also began to focus attention on Mwanza, the second largest town in the nation, because numerous youth had gone there for work and schooling. A right of occupancy was obtained and building was undertaken. In 1970 Pastor Naftali Birai, then manager of Mennonite Center in Musoma, went weekly to Mwanza to preach and to oversee the building work. Soon he committed the little flock to the first resident couple, Pastor Jona and Lea Mirari.

## Upgrading Shirati Hospital

In 1966 Shirati Hospital had a census of 28,394 outpatients, 2,034 inpatients, and 472 maternity patients. Plans were under way for expanding into additional types of medical care. All of these factors were cited to support the request sent to West Germany for funds to rebuild and upgrade the total plant.

When funds became available, new wards were built accommodating 104 beds. The total complex included consultation rooms, a laboratory, X-ray, surgery, and a two-story office block, as well as a large water tank and generator unit. This new plant was formally opened in 1972 by President Julius Nyerere. During the administration of Dr. Richard Weaver, a surgeon commonly known as *Mayom,* The Gentle One, the 1973 census of inpatients reached 3,029 and maternity patients, 1,247. Since other medical units had been established in the area, there were only 21,687 outpatients.

A portion of the new hospital was designed for leprosy patients requiring special treatment. Modern medicines had brought healing so that numerous patients had been able to return to their homes. Research had proven that leprosy is only mildly contagious, and that noninfected persons are not at risk if everyone in the family observes normal health practices, i.e., the use of soap in washing and bathing, and adequate cooking of foods. So a new pattern of treatment was established: the leprosy patient lives at home and goes to a dispensary each week for medication.

In view of this new approach, American Leprosy Mission provided funds for a leprosy control unit within the general hospital. The unit included a meeting hall (for the weekly clinic, for teaching sessions and for worship), wards providing 30 beds, a room for the making of prostheses, and another room for physical therapy. Mary Harnish had developed ways for making and fitting prostheses that helped many patients and also attracted staff members from other hospitals to learn her techniques.

When the leprosarium was closed in 1972,[3] of 400 patients only six were retained for further hospital care. During this same year a national committee was formed to guide and coordinate the treatment of leprosy. In 1972 the regional medical headquarters chose Shirati Leprosy Control Center to oversee leprosy treatment throughout Mara Region. A team of assistants was assigned to work with Dr. Glen Brubaker, the Shirati director. Each assistant was responsible for a given area. Along with the treatments, Brubaker supervised research to discover whether malaria might trigger one type of cancer.[4]

**Sharing the life of the whole church**

The Mennonites, who had been helped in many ways by other churches, also found opportunities to give help. They entered Tanganyika with the counsel and prayers of the then Tanganyika Missionary Council and the special help of Africa Inland Mission. Revival came to them through AIM and the Anglicans. In turn, the Mennonites participated in preaching and counseling ministries, and produced the *Messenger of Christ* and *Spiritual Songs,* both widely used in all denominations. During the crunch of educational expansion, the Anglicans, Lutherans, and Moravians helped the Mennonites with teachers. From 1963 to the present, the Mennonites helped staff CCT. Through the years this small Anabaptist group developed bonds of fellowship with each of the denominations; Mennonites sometimes served as catalysts and bridgebuilders.

Orie Miller and Elam Stauffer's 1934 contact with Tanganyika Missionary Council (reorganized in 1948 as Christian Council of Tanganyika) was prophetic. The missionaries in their day, and now Bishops Kisare and Sarya, have found in the council both resource and opportunities to serve. To make it easier for Bishop Kisare to place nationals in all leadership positions and to develop structures suitable to his people, the last of the older missionaries retired from Tanzania in the latter 60s. During this transition period the forum provided by CCT proved most helpful; it gave opportunity to relate to other heads of churches, and to share with leadership persons in the whole gamut of church ministries.

In CCT annual meeting the leaders learned to know one another and to fellowship together; as in breaking bread with another, each shared from his experience. As they counseled together, they often came to a common mind. Major issues were also discussed with Roman Catholic leaders—just as the missionaries had done, particularly matters in which it was helpful to speak to government with a united voice. From their side, government officers were also happy for opportunities to address the heads of churches and to receive their counsel. Usually a cabinet officer represented government; sometimes the president himself was the spokesman.

Through CCT the denominations worked together in many ways. The preparation of Bible lessons for primary, secondary, and Sunday schools has already been mentioned. Resource materials were prepared for youth groups and for home and family life ministries. Seminars for leaders were offered, covering all areas of church life. CCT arranged for gospel broadcasts on national radio and set up a schedule for the member churches. The Christian Union of Tanzania (known by its Swahili acronym, UKWATA) was organized to provide pastoral care and outreach for Christian youth in the secondary schools and teacher training colleges.

Since CCT had very limited financial resources, this large scope of work was possible only because the denominations seconded staff persons to the council and supported them. The Lutherans provided the general secretary and the coordinator for media ministries. The Anglicans provided the education secretary and the publications coordinator. The Moravians provided a leader for home and family life activities. The Mennonites provided a coordinator for relief and service ministries—Mahlon Hess in 1963, Harold Miller in 1965, and Phinehas Nyang'oro in 1970.

"The holy war" between the Roman Catholic and Protestant churches in the Lake Victoria area of Tanganyika was very intense in the 1950s, but by 1965 it was almost nil. The Holy Spirit used revival awakenings and the peacemaking approaches of Pope John XXIII to bring understanding and fellowship. One day Delbert Robinson opened his heart to Mahlon Hess regarding misunderstandings between Romans and Mennos in local school situations: "Brother, we are ambassadors of the same Savior; let us take the responsibility to help our adherents find reconciliation." As another expression of this fellowship, in numerous communities leaders of all the Christian denominations began to meet for prayer. In the larger towns they also hold joint services of public witness at Easter and Christmas. Mennonites have participated in all of these.

Sometimes Mennonite delegates left CCT meetings heavy with self-pity—on occasion in tears—because they did not have sufficient educational background to follow some of the discussions. Nevertheless, these same brothers were occasionally invited to preach in joint services or to address university students. They brought messages through which God touched hearts, and they received invitations to return. Hezekia Sarya, who had a good ministry in Dar es Salaam, served for a time as chairman of the interchurch fellowship.

# 9.

# DIFFICULTY, STRUGGLE, GROWTH, 1974-83

### The passing of Muganda

"Dear Mother, I'm not feeling well," said Ezekiel Muganda to his wife, Raheri Nyaburuma. "If God should take me, he will not forsake you; do keep on praying for our children." In Muganda's illness, his family left no stone unturned in seeking healing for him, but on January 4, 1974, the Lord took him. For the funeral, it was planned that his pastor colleagues should carry the coffin to the church, each to have a turn. As soon as they left the house, however, the crowd pressed in upon them. Everyone tried to get a turn.

People have many warm memories of Ezekiel Kaneja Muganda. During most of his fifteen years as evangelist he was based at Mugango. As co-worker with the missionaries, he often gave a helping hand in the outchurches. He served as pastor for twenty-four years, twenty of them in Musoma. He was a popular speaker in spiritual life conventions, much in demand among Mennonites and other denominations.

On the day when Idi Amin dropped bombs on Mwanza, most Musoma residents also fled to the countryside. But Muganda stayed. He said that should Musoma be attacked, he would go to the church to pray; should the church be destroyed, his body would be found in the posture of prayer.

The death of Muganda left a large vacancy. The church had lost an energetic evangelist, a beloved pastor, a trusted counselor, a vice-chairman, who held Luos and Bantus together. Everyone experienced what the tribal fathers expressed in a proverb: "When the big tree falls the little birds fly back and forth."

Others of the ordained had passed to their reward before him. Pastor Nathanael Nyamare's death in 1958, following a long illness, has already been noted. After a very short affliction Deacon Naftali Nyangi Chacha, also of Nyabasi, died in 1975. The death of Muganda, an outstanding leader, came like a warning that first-generation leadership

127

was approaching the end of its tenure. Since Muganda's death a total of eleven workers have passed, seven missionaries and four nationals (four died in 1983, including Muganda's widow, Raheri, and two in 1984).[1]

This becomes an appropriate point to offer thanks for, and to pay tribute to, six leaders who have each served TMC for 50 years: Paulo Chai Chemere, Zephania K. Migire, Daniel Opanga Oole, Naftali Magai Mugenyi, Simeon Magoti Sanjaga, and Bishop Zedekia M. Kisare. Several of these participated in the August 1984 jubilee celebrations, praising God and encouraging the younger leaders.

### Responding to national crises

Beginning about 1974 the nation experienced a series of problems which reduced national income. While the movement of people into village settlements was an investment in the future, it reduced agricultural production for a time. Then came the worldwide escalation of the cost of oil. Developing nations, like Tanzania, could afford only a limited supply. The Amin war erupted in 1978, at great cost to the Tanzanian government. Then came two consecutive years of famine.

These factors combined to bring great difficulties across the nation. Some factories had to reduce production, and others were closed. Transport became difficult. National income dropped because there was less grain and fewer manufactured goods to be sold. Few consumer goods were to be found in the shops. The consumer goods that did become available were hoarded or placed on black market. Even for staple foods one had to pay inflated prices and/or a bribe.

The shortage of fuel curtailed medical services. Shirati Hospital had to reduce visits to dispensaries, much as they regretted what this would mean to the mothers and children whom they had been serving. Surgical ministries and the use of X-ray had to be greatly reduced because there was little fuel to generate electricity.

During these difficulties TMC took steps to help its communities. When famine came, the bishops asked Mennonite Central Committee (MCC) for a shipment of wheat, which was divided among the four districts in Mara Region. As a pilot project in food production, a solar-powered irrigation project was undertaken by Dr. Glen Brubaker and MCC. Several church districts are attempting to begin other agricultural projects.

At Nyarero a simple vocational school, open to young men and women, was started by Naftali Birai and Gordon Peters. With limited resources they offered some training in agriculture, carpentry, masonry, and tailoring—to help youth become self-supporting.[2]

In the midst of shortages, many persons compromised their integrity to get what they needed. But many brothers and sisters have committed themselves to continue their walk with Jesus. They will not purchase on the black market, nor will they pay or receive a bribe. In this world of many shortages, whether of sugar, soap, kerosene, or other necessities, they testify that Jesus provides what they need and keeps them in peace. Even when the customary bus or bicycle is not available, they continue preaching the gospel. To reach unevangelized villages, some pastors walk 30 miles in a day.

**Faith that loves the enemy**

The Amin war involved the Mennonites of Mara Region. After a few bombs were dropped on Mwanza, people in the war zone were required to dig shelters. Morning and evening radio announcements kept them conscious of the conflict. Some brothers and sisters pondered deeply our Lord's command to love the enemy—how to do good instead of to destroy and to kill.

During World War II and since independence, some Mennonite youth had been enlisting in the army because it was a way to receive vocational training and to earn a salary. And when Idi Amin attacked Tanzania, some volunteered to fight against him, contrary to Mennonite understanding of the Scriptures.

The older leaders remembered the 1939-45 provisions for conscientious objectors—an opportunity to give evidence of faith and then be assigned work that would help the nation. So in 1983 TMC leaders were greatly encouraged when in a public meeting a national leader made a preliminary response to TMC's request for alternate service for Mennonite youth. He proposed that it was not possible to give blanket exemption, but that a way should be found for persons with genuine conscience.

TMC leaders, both ordained and lay, sometimes discuss how one loves the enemy in everyday life. They remember that in certain situations the missionaries hired night watchmen who sometimes carried indigenous weapons, and that, with violence on the increase, many present-day watchmen insist on carrying weapons.

The conviction to refrain from the use of weapons, however, is not new with Tanzanian Mennonites. A few remember the German Adventist missionary who, before Mennonites came, had lived near Shirati. In 1918 when the British victory in Tanganyika was finally acknowledged, he did not flee for safety. His testimony had been, "Love is more powerful than the gun." In the providence of God he was killed right there in his own house, the victim of a boot soldier who had been carried away by the flush of victory.

Some Mennonites had heard firsthand the testimonies of Kikuyu Christians as to how Jesus had provided for them during the Mau Mau conflict. They had refused the oath and any use of violence in the struggle to end white colonialism. Though many of their number had been brutally wounded and killed by Mau Mau warriors, Kikuyu Christian leaders refused the weapons offered by the British government to help guard their communities. Refusing Mau Mau violence and government violence, they chose a third way, Jesus' way of love. After the conflict it came to be widely recognized that the Mau Mau rebellion was overcome, not by the British military, but by the blood of hundreds of Kikuyu martyrs. Former Mau Mau guerrillas are now pastors.

Among the Mennonites, too, there were brothers who, in difficult experiences, had practiced the gospel of love. Elisha Meso was awakened one night hearing thieves taking his thirty-nine cattle from the corral. With his bow and arrows in hand, he got a good view of the thieves in the moonlight. Just as he was ready to release the first arrow, the Lord reminded him, "Do not kill." When he obeyed and put down his bow, other thieves armed with knives entered the house, taking everything of value. He fell to his knees, together with his wife and eleven children, thanking God that all of them were safe. In a few days the police were able to return the cattle and most of their personal effects.

Yakobo Wambura had taken his car to a garage for repairs. The mechanic had an apprentice who was very eager to learn to drive. He took the car without permission and, in a short distance, wrecked it. A policeman counseled Yakobo to take the matter to court, knowing that he could win compensation sufficient to buy a new car. "I am satisfied. The mechanic has promised to repair my car," Yakobo answered. "I want to be free to tell him about the love of Jesus, and also his helper."

### Shirati restored and Mugumu opened

Many, many people were treated in the Mennonite medical units, and some of them were also helped spiritually. In 1974 at Shirati 23,670 were treated, at Nyabasi 16,561, at Kisaka 13,250, at Bumangi 6,597, at Bukiroba 12,975, and at Mugango 13,732.

During the period 1975-78, however, the medical ministries at Shirati greatly deteriorated. There was a convergence of problems,

130

including shortage of water, insufficient staff, and inadequate supervision.

Several qualified persons were asked to visit the hospital, investigate the problems, and advise what might be done. TMC forwarded this report to the mission board requesting a major effort to restore good medical services. In 1979 the board fielded a mechanic, an administrator, and a doctor. Matters began to improve, as the records show. Whereas 15,532 had been treated in 1980, 21,725 were treated in 1982. Jeremia Okidi, chosen as medical secretary to oversee the total program, began to build good relationships between the hospital and the church. During this time, Enoka Kawira and Isaya Obiero were the hospital chaplains, successors to Yohana Waryuba. Yohana, now confined to his home by failing health, was still witnessing to all who came to him.

In 1974 a maternal child welfare campaign was launched by World Health Organization (WHO). The goal was to give early help to pregnant mothers and to inoculate babies against childhood diseases. Shirati Hospital undertook such ministry under the leadership of Verle Rufenacht. In time, there were fourteen clinics to be visited each month.

The Tanzanian government requested that Mennonite Church help establish a hospital in a district which did not yet have one. The health department had designated Bunda, but later substituted Mugumu, which was seen to have a greater need. The church's responsibility was to seek funding, to oversee the building, and to supply a doctor for five years. Mugumu Hospital was built because of the priority given it by President Nyerere and the hard work of Victor and Viola Dorsch and their team. Even though the international border was closed during the entire period, by presidential permission all building supplies were purchased in nearby Kenya and brought across the border.

The 80-bed hospital was formally opened in 1980 by President Nyerere. In 1982 Dr. Thomas Miller, the first medical officer, and his team treated 67,300 outpatients, 3,240 inpatients, and 396 maternity patients. The Mugumu congregation provides an excellent pastoral ministry, which includes weekly prayers with the staff, a worship service with the inpatients, and bedside counseling. Many of the hospital staff, both nurses and aides, are Christians.

An alternate project, a teacher training college with a capacity of 300, was provided to the Bunda community. CCT found a donor agency, and Joseph Bontrager, Daniel Wenger, and Daniel Mtoka gave oversight to the building operations. TMC has been invited to provide a chaplain and other senior staff persons to the college.

### Ordination of Bishop Sarya

A second bishop, Hezekia Nyamuko Sarya, was chosen on November 22, 1977. He was ordained on February 18, 1979, in a special service held in connection with a meeting of the ordained leaders.

Bishop Sarya was well known in Mennonite congregations, for he had served among them for 40 years. For 17 years he had been an energetic evangelist, zealous for the Lord. He made the most of his in-service training. In Bible school and in theological college, he had asked many questions and freely shared his own ideas. During his five years as a deacon and 18 as a pastor, he was a leader with vision, a vigorous preacher. After the death of Muganda, he became vice-chairman of TMC. Sarya and his faithful wife, Perusi, who has shared in all these assignments, have a family of twelve children living and others who died.

Bishop Kisare, who had been encouraged to call a bishop to work with him, entered upon this step very carefully because there was some unrest in the church. Throughout the nation tribal feelings were on the increase, affecting Mennonites also. Describing the state of the church, a brother said, "We slacked in praying and depended on human strategies." Discussions and planning revealed lack of unity. Many understood that the next step was to choose an assistant bishop. Others were determined that each bishop have his own diocese. After the choice of Brother Sarya, this lack of unity continued, and in the lapse of communication, even the ordination service could not be held on the scheduled date.

In time, two dioceses were formed, with a bishops' council to give leadership to the Bible school, Mennonite Center, and other joint projects. Later, without consultation with the conference bodies, the bishops' council was dissolved. Across the church there is support for the two dioceses, with, however, an eagerness for more fellowship and working together.

During this time when the church was at a low ebb spiritually, the Free Church of Africa sprang up in the Shirati area. This group gives much credence to African culture, particularly indigenous names and polygamy.

Many brothers and sisters are praying for renewal of unity among TMC leaders, for reconciliation at each point where there has been a breach. The emerging structures must be agreed upon and the constitution brought up-to-date. The magnitude of the tasks of nurture and evangelism, and the shortage of resources call for undertaking certain projects together, particularly leadership training.

'We will be patient and continue on," said one lay Christian. "We will not relax our hold on God." This brother had seen persons whom he trusted leave the church. He also regretted the rift in relationships. He remembered, however, how he had to bear with missionary shortcomings and that our Lord had used even human failure in the building of his church.

### Arusha, Tabora, Dodoma, Mara Region

In spite of the problems the church is facing, there is continuing concern for witness and growth. Mennonite adherents in Arusha had waited ten years from the time they first asked for a pastor until they received one. In 1976 Daniel Sigira was sent to begin weekly services and to oversee the building of a meetinghouse and a parsonage. At this time Wera Magangira was assigned to a dispensary at Kitete, Tabora, where he promptly began a small church. It has been said that wherever Wera goes he plants a church. In 1979 Phinehas Nyang'oro, assistant to the general secretary of CCT, was transferred to Dodoma. He had a counseling ministry with the Mennonites in the area but, since his duties involved much travel, he did not begin weekly worship. Then in 1983 evangelist K. J. Kaema started a Mennonite congregation there.

The children and pupils of TMC leaders are widely scattered. Whenever the senior church leaders reminisce, they talk about them: teachers, doctors, judges, engineers, administrators, cabinet members, and ambassadors. Some of them bear good witness for our Lord. All of them are glad to identify themselves as Mennonites.

There are Mennonite Christians in most of the urban areas across the nation, and some of them also are requesting a pastor and a meetinghouse for their towns. In response, the conference deputized two pastors to visit a series of towns in 1983. They were to go as far as Sumbawanga—for several years requests had come from there. Anticipating follow-up, one suggestion was that a pastor be set apart to minister to dispersed Mennonites. He would visit all such locations following an agreed-upon calendar, and the responses to his ministries could serve as a guide in assigning pastors and providing buildings.

More worship centers were opened in Mara Region during 1981-83. Noting that from 1968 to 1976 there had been a slump in evangelism, the 1976 conference session designated 1977 as a "year of evangelism." Six churches were opened in the following year. Although in the next two years only one was opened, in 1981 there were four, in 1982 there were six and in 1983, more than 12.

It is instructive to note that the opening of churches was slowed by each major event in the life of the church: revival, the call of the first pastors, the thrust of opening schools, national independence and church autonomy, the call of the first bishop, and the call of the second bishop and restructuring of the church. In every case a new bulge of growth has followed.

Seeing the increase in doors of opportunity, the church stepped up the recruitment of workers. From 1975-83 there were 16 pastors and 12 deacons ordained. (Because three of the deacons were later called to the pastorate, the real increase of deacons was only nine.) Of these pastors, seven are self-supporting, as were two pastors before them. The goal is to break out of the mind-set that believed pastors could not be called because there were no funds to support them.

Efforts are also being made to recruit lay Christians to teach religious instruction in the public schools. Because many classes have no Bible teachers, opportunities abound. For example, in the town of Musoma there are at least fifteen schools having two or more classes in each grade.

In recent years the gifts of women are being used in a larger way. Some are serving as elders and some as congregational leaders. This good trend also reflects a current problem. While in the 1940s congregations were comprised of twice as many men as women and in the 1950s the proportions became equal, today women are a strong majority.

### Nudges to witness beyond Tanzania

When the churches of Mozambique requested help in agriculture, in projects for increasing family income, and in resources for Bible teaching, Mennonite Central Committee responded, inviting TMC to partner with them in such efforts. Phinehas Nyang'oro participated in the exploratory visit. Although the church did not find it possible to send long-term workers to Mozambique, there are some who have begun to see our Lord's more distant harvest fields.

The Christian students in Mara Region, who hold an UKWATA convention each Easter season, in their 1983 meeting studied the theme, "Go into all the world and preach the gospel to every person." Four months later the Dar es Salaam congregation celebrated its 20th anniversary, focusing on this same text. The Rogoro District has moved beyond discussion. They joined the Bible Society of Tanzania to facilitate Bible distribution in their region and to have a part in making the Scriptures available around the world.

**"Clouds are the sign of rain"**

"We have really cooled off," said one sister. "We used to praise God with all our strength; now our praise is weak. I shared my testimony boldly even with strangers; now I'm silent. We warned those who left the way; now we are afraid of one another." From another congregation, a leader said, "We have robbed God of our offerings; we have neglected nurture of our youth and now some of them are being attracted to the new sects. We are praying for an awakening."

Our gracious Lord continues to move among Tanzania Mennonites, bringing fresh blessings. There is hunger for the Word of God. Out in the districts as many as 1,400 people come together in weekend spiritual life meetings. One notes that there is more life in the grass-roots congregations than in the centers where formal structures are strong. The Theological Education by Extension (TEE) courses taught by Victor and Viola Dorsch in the northern diocese have brought new life into those congregations. Church leaders are on the lookout for books and periodicals that help them in their work. Persons eager for revival would like to see *Messenger of Christ* revived. At Shirati revived persons continued to meet weekly for fellowship. Happily, there are a few youth among them. At other places the awakened ones seek fellowship wherever they meet another hungry heart. And throughout the church one finds dedicated parents who sing, read the Scriptures, and pray with their children each day.

God has confirmed his love through some healings. Having seen Edmond John pray for thousands in Dar es Salaam with miraculous healings following, Bishop Kisare pondered his cardiac asthma of seven years. Trusting that he could be healed, he returned to "the man of God" in Dar es Salaam. He was guided to spend a day in fasting, confessing any sinful attitudes, and fellowshiping with God. The next day he was to return for special prayer, looking to Jesus the Healer. When Kisare named his trouble, Edmond laid on hands and prayed in the name of Jesus. Kisare testified, "I was whole and at peace."

Kisare then invited Edmond to come to Musoma to preach repentance and to pray for the sick. When he came in 1975, many experienced Christ in a new way and many were healed physically. Nyerere Itinde, who had suffered stomach ulcers for fifteen years, was one of those who received healing. Two years later he was chosen chairman of the Nyabangi village settlement, a heavy responsibility he now carries without his former limitations. Each morning he prays, "Lord, give me a testimony for some hungry heart I will meet today."

135

At Nyarero dispensary a brother had been treated for two years, to no avail. Just when he had given up hope, Pastor Kabury visited him and asked, "Are you still trusting God, or has Satan gotten the victory?" When the brother confessed discouragement, the pastor urged, "Let's get on our knees and pray, and then God can give his answer." The brother's health began to improve.

God has blessed some brothers and sisters in the grace of giving, and has given them the desire to see others share the blessing. In the 1976 conference Nikanor Dhaje challenged the delegates that a church forty years old ought to be supporting its leadership. Nashon Nyambok told how a month of specific stewardship teaching in his district had resulted in a doubling of offerings. When Treasurer Birai announced his availability to lead stewardship seminars, several districts called him.

From 1977 onward there has been some growth in church offerings, despite the general economic decline. In one district four brothers who served in salaried positions returned the honoraria they had been given for church ministries. These gifts supported one more evangelist.

District councils have taken some initiatives without waiting for external financial aid. For example, the members of the Dar es Salaam congregation, who urgently need a meetinghouse, have designated one offering a month to a building fund. They hired an architect to prepare blueprints, purchased supplies, and put in a foundation. They continue presenting to God the large amount still needed to complete the project, and build as they can. Similarly in the Rogoro district, the Christians need a dwelling for their pastor and would like to provide a hostel for persons of limited means who come to the hospital. They have started the pastor's house, doing what they can and bringing their needs to God.

One senses God moving among the youth. "In some of the choirs I see an awakening among our youth, a sign of fresh revival," commented Bishop Kisare. The new life is reflected in hymns of praise and songs of admonition. Some choirs have begun singing Bible stories in the public markets. Occasionally, the choirs exchange visits with neighboring congregations, strengthening the church across denominational lines.

Youth are helping one another grow in Jesus. Even in schools where there are no teachers to encourage and help them, Christian youth gather each evening for prayer and meet in a weekly Bible study, following an UKWATA syllabus. And some of the older youth who work in factories, shops, and offices help one another in the struggles that confront them.

Some youth are ready to give themselves in church assignments. They know well the shortcomings in the church, and are aware that little financial support can be expected. However, they think of new approaches to pastoral work and evangelism. Some students have deep spiritual insights. George Nyambalya wrote this:

> The church is a creation which embodies the life of God, not a mere club or organization. The Living Christ, who gave himself to serve the church, is Head of this body. Therefore, leadership under him is different from worldly leadership: it is not authority over others, but fellowship and mutual helpfulness.

In this same vein Josiah Muganda, a retired teacher, said: "For a long time we have been receiving; now it is time for us to dedicate ourselves to serving others." He underscored the fact that TMC has been well known for its hospitals and schools, but the time has come to undertake some new ministries that respond to needs in today's Tanzania.

### "The light shines in the darkness"
The conflict between light and darkness was intensified at the passing of Susana Kisare on August 6, 1983; the boundaries between church and world became visible. Through the experience God's people received new measures of divine grace and were bound together in the Spirit. The bishop was eager that all duties during the watch, the funeral, and the days of mourning be carried by God's people, the new tribe, not the traditional family because it included many unbelievers.

The women of the church stepped in immediately. Soon after Mama's passing, they surrounded the body singing gospel songs. Their singing served to temper the wailing and commotion of those still in darkness. Around the clock they sang in relay, from Friday night until the funeral Monday forenoon—witnessing to peace and joy in the homegoing of one of God's saints. When not singing they helped with the cooking and hospitality.

Sharing the bishop's concerns, the church leaders participated with him in decision-making. They assigned persons to look after the guests and established a hospitality fund to cover expenses. They arranged all the details of the funeral service. In a showdown between traditional family and God's family, church leaders supported the bishop that burial should be at the church, not in the family village, and that the grave not be closed in traditional Luo fashion—ways of signifying a total break with the spirit world. Cattle would not be ceremonially driven across the grave; rather, each relative and friend could place a stone on the grave to honor the deceased.

Susana had been "mother of the whole of TMC," and in the funeral crowd of 2,000 every tribe was represented. In marked contrast to the two days of wailing and occasional tumult, the whole church compound was quiet. The grace of God covered the assembly, inside and outside the church, enabling Pastor Nashon Nyambok and Bishop Hezekia Sarya to preach with joy and liberty. In a testimony Bishop Kisare thanked church and community for the moral support and material help given to him. He testified that his time of mourning had become like a spiritual life convention in which he was strengthened in the inner man.

A personal representative of President Julius Nyerere brought condolences. Leaders from other denominations and spokesmen for the family paid tribute. Joseph Shenk, who had just finished editing the bishop's autobiography, paid tribute to Susana and reminisced on his associations with the family. Following the service, messages of condolence arrived from the Lancaster Mennonite bishops, from Eastern Mennonite Board, and from Mennonite General Assembly, then in session at Bethlehem, Pennsylvania, celebrating the 300th anniversary of the first permanent Mennonite settlement in North America.

People left the burial service thanking God for the grace they had seen in Bishop Kisare and remembering his request for continued prayer support.

# 10.

# THE PILGRIMAGE CONTINUES

**TMC present in God's caravan** (a meditation)
*Our God acts in history, calling humans to pilgrimage,*
*bringing together that innumerable multitude*
*who will people his eternal kingdom,*
*servants of his ongoing purposes.*

*God the Father created man with reason and conscience.*
*He called people, in families, to walk with him:*
*Adam and Eve, Noah and family, Abraham and Sarah,*
*Moses and sister Miriam, David and the prophets.*
*Each made a faith response,*
*and God, through thousands of years,*
*called forth the family of faith*
*through whom the Savior would come;*
*he readied the world civilizations*
*in which he would plant his church.*

*God the Son became man.*
*He came to persons of faith:*
*Zechariah and Elizabeth, Joseph and Mary, Simeon and Anna.*
*For thirty-three years he made God visible among people,*
*a pilgrimage of life, death, and resurrection,*
*training people of faith to continue his work.*

*God the Spirit lives within man.*
*He came upon the apostles and believers*
*constituting them the body of Christ,*
*his continuing presence in the world.*
*Because his church, in its humanity,*
*sometimes compromised, sometimes denied him,*

*he disciplined and purified her.*
*Through two millennia he found responsive persons*
*through whom he goes on building the pilgrim community:*
*Polycarp, Justin Martyr, Perpetua, Tertullian, Chrysostom,*
*Maximilian, Augustine, St. Patrick, Photius,*
*Bernard of Clairvaux, Peter Waldo, Francis of Assisi,*
*Savas of Serbia, John Wycliffe, John Huss, Jerome Savonarola,*
*Martin Luther, Ulrich Zwingli, Conrad Grebel,*
*Francis Xavier, Nicholas von Zinzendorf, Susanna Wesley,*
*John Wesley, William Carey, Mary Slessor, Seraphim of Savov,*
*John Henry Newman, Florence Nightingale, Cardinal Lavigerie,*
*Dwight Moody, John S. Coffman, Mary Denlinger,*
*Elam Stauffer, Marwa Kisare, Phebe Yoder, Billy Graham,*
*John XXIII, Athenagoras I, Elizabeth O'Connor,*
*Festo Kivengere, Mother Teresa, Paulus Mar Gregorius, Luis Palau. . . .* [1]

*Through a continuous line of faith*
*the gospel came to East Lake.*
*Tanzania Mennonite Church,*
*heir to all that has gone before,*
*has the Holy Scriptures,*
*divinely called leaders,*
*her own patterns of worship.*
*With fellow pilgrims she tells the Good News,*
*inviting those who have not yet heard*
*to join the caravan,*
*to walk as pilgrims of faith.*

## The initiatives of God

Through God's initiatives throughout fifty years, TMC came into being.

*The Spirit of God moves ahead of the church, preparing those whom he purposes to use.* Marwa, Wambura, and Opanga have shared how God first spoke to them—from 1915 onwards—preparing them for the gospel. During the same period he called missionaries. Phebe Yoder sensed God's call to Africa twenty-one years before the church approached her. The writer, his wife, and other missionaries have had similar experiences.

Local persons helped Marwa, Wambura, and Opanga make their initial responses of faith. When the Mennonites arrived, Daniel Opanga and Joseph Agunya had been leading the church at Alicho for nine years.

Ezekiel Muganda was an evangelist in charge of an AIM congregation. Zedekia Kisare was a baptized Christian and Nashon Nyambok had quietly made his commitment. From the beginning the missionaries could relate to a few local believers, studying the Word of God with them, reaching out to others.

In the evangelization of Africa there are a number of places where God first used local messengers and then brought missionaries, according to Bishop Sundkler. In this way God reminded the expatriates that he is Lord of the harvest; he had been present all the while, preparing the local people. In time these missionaries could look back and see that indeed they were carrying forward what God himself had begun. Further, their task was not only to evangelize and nurture, but also to grow personally in a believer group in a different culture, experiencng new dimensions of the gospel.

*God prepares his church for a new step of obedience by calling some of his people to pray.* The offerings that began coming in 1926 were evidence that some persons were asking God to send messengers to Africa. Some students at Eastern Mennonite School felt the same burden. John and Ruth Mosemann were part of such a prayer group in 1930. Through many prayers in the 1930-40s, East Africa was prepared for revival. After special prayer the churches of Mugango-Majita and Shirati unamimously discerned their first pastors. Later, after fresh repentance and prayer, a Bantu-Nilotic impasse was overcome, and unitedly the church called a Nilotic as their first bishop.

*Each changed life is a miracle.* The drunkard and the adulterer become faithful husbands and fathers; the thief becomes a trusted custodian; the proud, sharp-tempered missionary becomes a gentle counselor. Likewise the blending of temperaments and cultures into a harmonious congregation is evidence that Jesus is present and in charge.

*God plants believers in families, bridging personal, tribal, and cultural gaps.* The new believer, making a costly break with the community of which he had been a part, is received into the new family of God. Within the family he finds brothers and sisters from other tribes, other nations, other ways of life. The unity they find is a gift from Jesus.

Even though we Mennonites, missionaries and Tanzanians, shared food together more than our peers in other denominations, we often criticized and hurt one another. But when we faced our sins and came afresh to Jesus, beneath his cross we found each other. We were truly one, free to share with each other: material blessings and spiritual insights, person to person and church to church. We therefore continue to need each other. Both TMC and Lancaster Conference are eager for such fellowship to continue.

*The Spirit of God is always seeking to revive his people.* Like the wind, he moves where he chooses. Through the Moody revivals the Spirit called the first overseas missionaries from among North American Mennonites. Decades later he prepared persons in England and in India to minister in revival with a second generation of Mennonite missionaries in an East African setting. Revival came to Mugango, to Nyabasi, and to Shirati, when missionaries and nationals humbled themselves before God and restored their broken relationships. And when they depended on the initial revival experience and lost their vitality, Jesus came to them afresh, teaching them how to wash one another's feet, keeping clean for the journey. It is encouraging that at this writing the Spirit has moved a few to pray for a fresh visitation of revival in Tanzania and in the United States.

*God uses faltering humans to plant new churches.* Pioneer John Mosemann continues to express his gratitude "for the unforeseen and the *abundantly above* blessing that has followed through fifty years.... We were more colonialistic than we realized; we were paternalistic and failed to show respect for the indigenous culture. We frequently deplored our lack of anthropological training. God has overruled so much; we rejoice in what he has accomplished through vessels of clay."

*God corrects and develops the concepts and methods of his servants.* Just as he accepts each new believer as he is and leads him into fuller truth, so also he accepts the new missionary with whatever cultural and personal biases he may have. But, through relating to peers, through the need to be relevant to the host culture, and through confrontations with the powers of darkness, God corrects his false and inadequate ideologies and methodologies and develops them. The changes experienced by Lancaster Conference, noted below, illustrate this.

### Obligations on TMC and Lancaster Conference

The initiatives of God place obligations upon those who receive the blessings, both the Tanzania church and Lancaster Conference (LMC).

1. *The sacrifice of thanksgiving:* God has brought a new church into being. In this he called many of us to participate with him, enlarging our hearts and our circles of fellowship. We must not fail to respond with praise. There is the legend of two angels who collected prayers. The angel who gathered requests for blessing had an overflowing basket, while the one who collected thanks had very few prayers in his basket. In the past

fifty years we have sent many requests to God. May our jubilee celebrations spark ongoing responses of gratitude and thanks-living.

Tanzania Mennonite Church celebrated her jubilee on August 4-5, 1984, at Shirati, an event planned as "an offering of praise from those whose lives were touched by the mission." Of the 5,400 present, many had traveled on foot. In the crowd were more than a dozen former missionaries and six representatives of Lancaster Conference and its mission board. The president of Tanzania, Julius K. Nyerere, and his wife, Maria, were special guests of the bishops.

A congregational hymn, "Rock of Ages," set the tone for the event: praise for past blessings, a present renewal of covenant, and faith for the future. The acts of God in forming the church were recited by seven youth choirs and highlighted in a humorous perceptive skit by the Shirati women. Tools for telling the story to future generations were formally presented: a pillar commemorating Elam Stauffer at the first campsite, a 50th-anniversary plaque in the wall of the first building erected in 1934, the Swahili edition of this book, and Bishop Kisare's autobiography. Addresses by Donald Jacobs and Josiah Muganda helped the church begin to reflect on her heritage and to project for the future. Two liberal offerings reflected the joy and enthusiasm of the participants.

Lancaster Conference is preparing its response to the jubilee, events to be held in July 1985, with TMC leaders as special guests. Our "offering of praise" is first of all for revival. Revival sent LMC to Tanzania in 1934, and the East African revival spilled back to us in deliverance from sins, breaking down barriers and opening new vistas of fellowship and witness. Through revivals, Lancaster Conference has been changed from within.

We also give thanks that God has been correcting our inadequate ideologies and methodologies. We started with the assumption that to give priority to evangelism, ministries such as medicine and education must be severely restricted. However, in fellowship with Tanzanian brothers and sisters we learned to minister to body, mind, and spirit as one of the foundations for a self-sustaining church. We also began to learn that Christian presence is itself a ministry.

We had set out to build a self-propagating, self-governing, self-supporting church. We had assumed that in some ways TMC would be different from LMC, and that Lancaster should monitor TMC's major decisions. We needed to learn that the emerging church is a sister church, not a child, and to allow her to establish her own molds, expressing the gospel in her own situation. This also set us free to begin learning from our national brothers and sisters: for example, that people are more important than schedules and programs.

We had assumed that separation from the world included separation from churches different from us. But God used other churches to lead us to East Lake, to guide us in being helpful in difficult marriage situations, to lead us to experience Jesus in revival, and to help us develop TMC's schools and medical programs. As we accepted our brothers and sisters from other churches, he also opened larger doors of witness to us.

We had carried with us our long-standing fear of participation in political processes. But when a new nation was being born, and Christians were the best-trained persons in the community—when the community asked persons with strong moral principles to be their leaders—it was clear that Christians had a responsibility to help affect and shape the new political structures. It was also clear that Christian nonresistance places certain limitations on political roles.

Fifty years of partnering with TMC have helped us begin to distinguish the gospel and its imperatives from Pennsylvania Dutch patterns for expressing the gospel. We have learned to allow national churches to evaluate their own cultures, to discern what is helpful in their walk of faith and what needs the judgment of the gospel. God has helped us take the same approach in our home mission efforts. In addition, many among us have learned how to respond responsibly to change within our Lancaster Conference culture.

Bringing our Pennsylvania Dutch culture under the judgment of the gospel is important. But we have greater cultural problems—our total Western worldview and the political and economic institutions under which we live. Just as our Tanzanian brothers had to refuse to participate in some of the established practices of their communities, we will need to say "no" to more than joining the armed forces. Just as our brothers in communist and socialist settings have to say "no" to some of the demands placed on them, so persons of faith are going to have to say "no" to many of the demands of current materialistic capitalistic democracy. Unless we do so, we will discover that we are standing with the enemies of God, participating in the oppression of our brothers and sisters in developing countries. Saying "no" to the economic injustices of our own culture is costly, as a later segment will show.

We can give thanks for a new set of values, learned in missions involvement. Fellowship and exchange with brothers and sisters from TMC helps liberal givers realize, as longtime EMBMC treasurer Ira J. Buckwalter, said: "What we have given to missions was the best financial

144

investment we ever made." Most of our congregations and many of our families have also given persons in missions/service assignments and have been enriched by the spiritual growth in the workers. Many have experienced special answers to prayer.

We must give thanks for God's gift of leaders. The mission in Tanganyika was launched on the initiative of our Lancaster bishops. Through these fifty years the bishops have participated in every meeting of the mission board, guiding the missionaries and counseling with the Tanzania church. When official policy and needs of the emerging church were in tension, they stood with the missionaries in the gap. Together they thrashed out the issues, absorbing the blows. Bishops shared with the board in evaluating new calls that came and in each decision to enter twenty additional countries. All these experiences have contributed to the quality of leadership our conference enjoys today.

Bishop Raymond Charles, who gave more than twenty years in leadership of our mission board, is one example of how involvement in overseas mission enriched ministry to the home churches. A number of years ago a senior bishop commented, "Where would Lancaster Conference be today if we had not experienced the blessings and disciplines of participation in worldwide missions?"

For such enlargement and enrichment of spirit, let us offer "the sacrifice of praise." A recital of events and discernment of purposes is not enough; let us present our bodies as a living sacrifice.

2. *Mutual upbuilding:* What God has done in us and through us obligates Lancaster Conference and TMC to help one another grow. During the Shirati jubilee, Bishops Kisare and Sarya invited our continued fellowship and help. Josiah Muganda spelled out some of the specifics. He saw TMC continuing to grow and to scatter, needing much nurture. He pointed out that the Tanzanian government is calling the churches to new initiatives in providing leadership for educational and medical institutions. Noting that man has been given dominion over the created world, Josiah underscored Christian responsiblity in working at the problems of hunger, poverty, water supply, and renewable supply of firewood, all as part of the church's ministry. He appealed for some capital and some people. He also asked for more opportunities for interaction between the Mennonites across Africa and for provision for higher education in Africa for all Anabaptist groups.

At present we have opportunity to give significant help to the Tanzania church and nation. Such opportunity, however, may not always continue. Should the door for close interaction sometime be closed,

TMC will find her way. Our Lord who planted the church will not abandon her. Meanwhile let us do what we can.

We of LMC also need help from TMC. Some of us are in danger of drowning in riches while around us society is decaying in self-indulgence, surfeiting, and pleasure-seeking. We tell ourselves that our prosperity is the special blessing of God. But our brothers in Tanzania remember that United States of America took land from the native Americans and built some of its agriculture and industry on slave labor. They know that America's minorities still provide a pool of cheap labor. They see the multinational corporations pay too little for labor and raw materials, and demand too much for what they have to sell. They are aware that, beyond the benefits the developing nations receive, the world economic system siphons from them and gives an unfair share of benefits to the industrial nations.

Trusting in the god of military might to preserve these advantages—in the guise of liberty—many Americans are satisfied for an inordinate share of national income to be expended on armaments. In this kind of nation God has called us to be "salt" and "light." We need the prayers of our brothers and sisters around the world—that we be released from the bondage that requires us to have a comfortable life. We need brotherly admonition as to how we can best give our witness. Has the time come for Anabaptists to migrate again?

Let us face the fact that the industrial nations are growing richer at the expense of the developing nations. Soon after Tanzanian independence, Julius Nyerere was thanking a donor nation for a financial aid package. Then he added, "Did you think of it?—if your businessmen would pay us two cents more per pound for sisal fiber, that would add up to more than this grant. And what is more, my government would not have the problem of deciding who should benefit from these funds. The persons who work and prepare sisal would benefit."

This gives us some insight into why the income of Lancaster Conference members grows much faster than the income of TMC constituency. Of course we have exceptional soil and good rainfall. But the profits of the Western industrial economy—in part from Africa, Asia, and Latin America—trickle down to us and, as one perceptive American bishop said forty-five years ago, "they are stained with blood." His admonition: "We dare not enrich ourselves from an economy with military foundations; we must use these extra dollars to feed the hungry and preach the gospel." In his comment the bishop was recognizing that a few Christians cannot overnight correct world economic patterns—

146

there are many interrelated social and political problems. What he was laying on our consciences is that we do control the resources that come to us.

Refusal to enrich ourselves includes *learning to live with less.* Our health will be the better, and we will have more to share.

*One tenth is the beginning for giving,* not the end! After our basic needs have been provided, the remainder should be directed to the hungry and suffering, meeting their needs and sharing the gospel. We who have the mind of Christ can share resources and power with the younger churches. In this way the church can model what the nations ought to do. Currently Lancaster Conference is channeling $2 million a year to churches in overseas countries, strengthening the ministries of 22,000 brothers and sisters in emerging churches. But we are not yet giving as the Lord has prospered.

*We must speak up for correction of the unjust structures:* in conversation with brothers and in the marketplace, in "letters to the editor," and in approaches to those who shape our laws and economy. En route to Tanzania I had opportunity to share Nyerere's suggestion with a corporate lawyer from one of the large multinationals. "Let's face it," he said, "with our corporations the bottom line is profit!" He was ready to consider his Christian responsibility to speak to that very issue. But corporations cannot change so long as the masses of people operate by the same principle.

Our first responsibility, therefore, is *to give ourselves in evangelism and in praying for revival.* Revival saved England from the kind of bloody revolution that France suffered, and revival spilled over to America. Revived persons, Wilberforce and Finney, spearheaded the movement which eventually freed the slaves. In our day, the Peace Corps approach to correcting imbalances was a good beginning. But until a multitude of converted people move out in genuine identification with the poor, the deepest needs of the people will go unmet. Let us continue to pray for revival.

The moral decay, increase of crime, political corruption, economic difficulties, and nuclear danger are all related. They grow, out of the addiction of men to material gain. If the present imbalanced structures continue, God will once again raise up the poor and bring down the rich. Unless there is worldwide revival, we face terrible judgments.

In this dangerous situation there are small but significant things we must do: we can pray, give our offerings, be just in all our dealings, and put ourselves on record for the correction of social injustices, praying for grace and willingness for the sacrifices such changes will require. A few dedicated persons will make a difference.

In *Idols of Our Time*,[2] Dutch economist and parliamentarian Bob Goudzwaard warns against the idols of prosperity, revolution, nationalism, and power (to guarantee security). He calls on Christians to take critical steps of sacrificial obedience; to be the first to repent of complicity in these idolatries. He points out that the little steps we take, acts of love and justice, are a declaration of faith in God, on the basis of which he works in society. For example, when the little boy gave his lunch to Jesus, our Lord then multiplied the resources and organized the channels for feeding 5,000.

We are not mere crusaders to change society; we are pilgrims passing through a messed-up world. Christ in us throws light on the real issues. He sensitizes our consciences and uses us to touch other consciences. As God leads, we take "the critical steps of sacrificial obedience," the acts of love and justice that release his power against the principalities and powers that control this present world. On the cross our Lord absorbed all that Satan brought against him; he rose again and reversed the course of history. Through his people he now seeks to reverse the course of evil in society, in United States and Tanzania. As we pray for such revival, let us give ourselves anew to him.

3. *Fresh initiatives in evangelism:* Our third response should be some new efforts to spread the gospel. Five times in his last forty-three days Jesus charged his followers that everywhere they go they are to make disciples. He had not written a book to leave with them, but he had shared his life with the Twelve, demonstrating the way and teaching them. He had prepared them for his continuing presence in the Spirit, and through them would put the story on record for us. Our Lord has set the pace. As his people we must bear witness in every place, planting clusters of believers.

An important way to mark this jubilee would be some new step in evangelism. Since 1949 TMC and Lancaster Mennonites have been attempting joint efforts in evangelism. Mbulu did not open to us. A joint project in Somalia did not prove possible. A way to go together to Mozambique, or some other place, has not yet been found.

However, LMC could help TMC respond to calls from within Tanzania. In 1983 a few Tanzanian brothers asked about the possibility for Lancaster-TMC joint evangelistic efforts in North America. In the Shirati celebrations, Don Jacobs appealed to TMC to help evangelize Europe and North America. He cited the sad decline of faith in the industrial nations in other parts of the world as compared to the rapid growth of churches in Africa.

In today's world, the proper approach in many places and situations is by interracial international teams. By carrying the gospel together to new places, the fellowship between TMC and Lancaster could grow.

Our goal in recounting TMC history has been to help both conferences prepare for the tasks ahead. When TMC youth began to write jubilee songs, the recurring theme was evangelism. The choir from Magoto, Nyabasi, dedicated themselves to the task:

> It is the responsibility of youth:
> let us put our minds to it;
> we still have strength
> to do the work of the Lord.
> Let us accept to be sent
> into the harvest of the Lord,
> the harvest is abundant.
> I call to all of you youth,
> to you fathers,
> to you mothers,
> let us note from where we have come.
> Let us give thought to our progress,
> the places where we have had victory;
> let us look at our failures,
> the places where we have come short.
> Let us fix in our minds
> that our responsibility here on earth
> is to preach the gospel,
> that many be saved.

We Mennonites, like other Christians, often nudge each other to be more diligent in witnessing. There is an old Swahili proverb, "A slave talks, but a free man acts." It is easy to talk, but the responsible person gets to work.

Through prayer for revival, bringing people to Jesus and planting them in fellowships, God will have opportunity to bring TMC up a seventh mountain in its pilgrimage of faith, and to give Lancaster Mennonites a new burst of growth.

**Keeping in step** (a meditation)

*The pilgrimage of faith—*
*of "no-people" becoming "the people of God"—*
*has become visible in Marwa, Wambura, Opanga*
*and the brothers and sisters of TMC.*
*They responded to God's initiatives:*
*they received the Savior*
*and took their place in the family of faith;*
*they exercise their gifts in the body,*
*looking for God's consummation in history.*

*The pilgrimage is possible*
*because Jesus Christ paid a great price:*
*he stepped down from the glory and authority of heaven;*
*he became one with those whom he would save,*
*a servant, meeting every kind of need.*
*In every step he was obedient to God,*
*even to absorbing violence, dying on a cross.*
*Therefore God resurrected him.*

*The caravan of faith will grow*
*only when Jesus in each disciple pays the price:*
*stepping down,*
*relating to people,*
*serving human need,*
*total obedience to God,*
*dying to selfish desires and absorbing hurts,*
*trusting God for resurrection.*

*Jesus, our Savior and Lord,*
*walks at the head of the caravan,*
*He has nurtured LMC and TMC to the present;*
*the future is in his hands.*
*As he explained through his parable:*
*Using men, he causes his kingdom to grow.*

> *The kingdom of God*
> *is as if a man should scatter seed upon the ground,*
> *and should sleep and rise night and day,*

*and the seed should sprout and grow,*
*he knows not how.*
*The earth produces of itself,*
*first the blade,*
*then the ear,*
*then the full grain in the ear.*
*But when the grain is ripe,*
*at once he puts in the sickle,*
*because the harvest has come*
*( Mark 4:26-29)*

# 11.

# NEW PERSONS, THE FAMILY OF GOD
## John H. Mosemann

The apostle Paul, in his letter to the Ephesians, chapter 2, sets out the story of every true Christian and of every true church. It is therefore the picture of Mennonites in America and in Tanzania.

As a missionary, Paul preached in Ephesus and planted the church. Later he wrote this letter to help believers grow in understanding of their Christian walk. He declared that although Jews and Gentiles had differences, they had the same spiritual needs. As God saw them, they were dead. They were shaped by the world around them, in rebellion against God, slaves of unholy desires of the flesh and mind.

Only the power of new life could change this condition. That life was made available by the mercy and love of God. He sent his Son to show the extent of his love. Jesus spent his life helping those in need, showing the true nature of God, and was crucified for it. But God raised him from the dead. He did more. He gave new life to all who trusted him for salvation. This was a gift, no one deserved it; therefore, no one could boast of his own merit. Our only boast is that God has made us his children. Our praise dare not be words alone, but acts which prove we are his children.

There is a second theme in this chapter. Jews and Gentiles were both estranged from God. Since they are now reconciled to God, their estrangement from each other is ended. When the walls which separate people from God are removed, the walls which separate them from each other also come down. People who were alienated, for whatever reason, are joined in Christ.

In his cross, Jesus removed all enmities. He declared peace among all peoples. The war is over. All that divided mankind is gone. By the Spirit we have been led along the same path to God.

There is more. Christians, no matter what their origins, are now one family with all the saints. They are members of God's household. They are parts of one building of which apostles and prophets are the foundation, and Jesus is the chief cornerstone. Every part is joined to him as one brick upon another; together we become a dwelling place for God.

Until now I have been telling the story of the Ephesian believers. These words also describe Mennonites who carried the gospel and those in Tanganyika who received it. Like the Jews, our Mennonite ancestors were highly privileged. They found the way of life 460 years ago in Europe. Then God led them through hard experiences. Many were killed for their faith. Many others came to America to find new land and opportunity. Although it was difficult to establish new homes in a strange land, they prospered. They built homes, churches, and schools.

God's disciplines prepared them to leave their homes again, not because of persecution, but to share their faith. Some missionaries went to India; others went to Argentina. In 1934 God led some of us from Lancaster Conference to you in Tanganyika, East Africa.

We came to you because God sent us. We knew little about your people or land. We had little understanding of the religion which controlled your lives. We must have seemed proud, even superior, because of our religion, ancestry, learning, and wealth. We repent of such attitudes and conduct. The fact is that we have the same roots that you have, that the Ephesians had. American Mennonites also had to accept God's life as a gift. We had to experience that the way of salvation begins with repentance and faith, and issues in new life in Christ. We came to Tanganyika because we had tasted the love and mercy of God and wanted you to join us in this pilgrimage of freedom and life.

In our zeal to have you become new persons and a new tribe in Jesus Christ, did we seem to reject everything African? Did we fail to keep clear that we wanted to let God use your gifts—to build his Tanzanian Church with Tanzanian materials? Forgive us for this wrong! The only likeness to the American church which you needed was that God should be the Builder, and Christ the Foundation. Both you and we, after we were no people, have become God's people (1 Peter 2:10).

It was not easy to break through barriers which divided us, even though we were missionaries bringing the gospel to you. But the message of the New Testament is clear: there may be differences among Christians, but these may not become barriers between them. We are different in origins, cultures, economic and religious backgrounds. But our common sinfulness before God, and our common new life in Christ, lift us above all barriers. The miracle of becoming one people in Christ from different tribes and nations, builds bridges between Americans and Africans, between North Mara and Southern dioceses, between Tanzania and Kenya, between church leaders and members. Since God lives in you and in us, we are brothers and sisters. God is our common Father. No relationship can be closer.

Praise God, in his grace he has called us from our emptiness and confusion to be his people together. Accept your oneness with us, as we accept our oneness with you. Let us allow the Spirit of God to lead us in our faith commitment to him and to each other. If we do not live in this unity which the Spirit has created, we cannot remain the people of God; instead we will become a people of rivalries. May God continue to possess Tanzania Mennonite Church as a people redeemed, living in the glory and will of God.

# II. HISTORICAL OVERVIEW OF TANZANIA MENNONITE CHURCH KANISA LA MENNONITE TANZANIA

Explanatory notes:

    a. Hereunder each church has been assigned a number, which also appears on the regional or national map in the photo section, showing its location.

    b. Churches which discontinued are not listed.

    c. *indicates a person who has not continued in the faith.

## A. North Mara Diocese, by districts

### 1. KAMAGETA

**Congregations and first leaders**:

| | | | |
|---|---|---|---|
| 1 | Migeko | 1925 | Apolo N. Onyango |
| 2 | Alicho | 1926 | Daniel Opanga Oole, Joseph Agunya |
| 3 | Tobache | 1954 | Joshafat Waga |
| 4 | Osiri | 1955 | Dishon Ngoya, Nashon Owido |
| 5 | Ryagoro | 1958 | Daudi Odoyo |
| 6 | Nyambori | 1958 | Joshafat Ombalo |
| 7 | Mariwa | 1961 | Sospita O. Waga |
| 8 | Kitembe | 1964 | Zablon A Oyucho |
| 9 | Nyambogo | 1967 | Salmon L. Kaler |
| 10 | Ingiri | 1968 | William Ragol |
| 11 | Panyako | 1973 | Andrea A. Ojuang' |
| 12 | Nyamasanda | 1978 | Daudi Wade |

*This district was formed in 1966; prior to this oversight was from Shirati.*

**Ordained leaders**:

| | |
|---|---|
| Zephania K. & Rusabella Migire | 1955–72 |
| Dishon M. & Mikal Ngoya | 1955–77 |
| Narkiso N. & Peris Odhiambo | 1972– |
| Manaen N. & Kezia Wadugu | 1978– |

*Council secretary*: Andrea A. Ojuang'

**Other leaders and elders**: Hezron Obuombe, Nashon Adera Arwa, Barak Orondo, Sitakus Obuombe, Jemsi Aron, Daudi Wadugu, Margret Ragot, Jemsi Odero, Aska Hezron, Yokabeti Harun, Doris Owele.

### 2. MORI

**Congregations and first leaders**:

| | | | |
|---|---|---|---|
| 180 | Omuga | 1949 | Isaya Obiero |
| 181 | Kibachiro | 1950 | Nathanael R. Nyamare |
| 182 | Nyakoba | 1952 | Narkiso N. Odhiambo |
| 183 | Kiterere | 1955 | Narkiso Magati |
| 184 | Ligero, (Buturi) | 1955 | Harun Ndiege |
| 185 | Utegi | 1958 | Nashon Nyambok |
| 186 | Chereche | 1975 | Daniel Mwita |
| 187 | Tingirime | 1983 | Daniel Mwita |

*Oversight from Nyabasi until 1966 and from Tarime until 1983, when brought together into a district.*

**Ordained leader**:

| | |
|---|---|
| Gershon Ayoo & Dorina Mbudi | 1983– |

## 3. NYABASI

**Congregations and first leaders:**

| | | |
|---|---|---|
| 40 Nyarero | 1940 | Clinton Ferster, Noah Mack |
| 41 Nyakunguru | 1946 | Yeremia Kabury |
| 42 Kangaliani | 1948 | Alexander Makorere |
| 43 Kyoruba (Bukira) | 1948 | Nathanael R. Nyamare |
| 44 Mangucha | 1950 | Yeremia Kabury |
| 45 Kemakorere (Mang'ong'o) | 1968 | Nathanael R. Nyamare, Naftali N. Nyakibari |
| 46 Masanga | 1973 | Marko Mwita |
| 47 Gamobaso | 1977 | Stefano Matiko |
| 48 Kelende | 1978 | Stefano Matiko |
| 49 Kewanja | 1978 | Stefano Matiko |
| 50 Kegonga | 1983 | James Nyantondo |
| 51 Magoto | 1983 | Lawrence C. Wambura |

*Formed from this district were Tarime District 1966 and Mori District 1983.*

**Ordained leaders:**

| | |
|---|---|
| Noah & Muriel Mack | 1940–45, 1949–52 |
| Simeon & Edna Hurst | 1940–64 |
| Robert & Florence Keener | 1953–54, 1960–61 |
| Nathanael Rhobi & Dina Nyamare | 1956–58 |
| Yusufu & Ana Wambura | 1956– |
| Yeremia Marara & Esta Kabury | 1959– |
| Naftali Nyangi & Damari Chacha | 1960–75 |
| Naftali & Elizabeth Birai | 1969, 1981– |

*Council secretary:* Simion Zablon

**Other leaders and elders:** Samweli Maitarya, Timotheo Mohabe, Samuel Ngoga*, Amon Mekere*, Yoshua Magige, Filipo Mwita*, Eliya Kuchenga*, Nicolaus Waibe, Yoeli Moherai, Elias Chacha, Simeon Marwa Nyakibari, Stefano Maginga Nyakibari, Zabron Waibe, Paulo Hula*, Caleb Randa, Raphael Magoti, Isaya Mrimi*, Petro Nyangi*, Sospater Magoiga*, Joseph Mbota*, William Gomba, Zakaria Mwita, Eliudi Sasati, Roda Mtatiro, Durusila N. Machambiri, Sara Wairungu, Zablon Wankogere, Harun Chacha, Marko Baru, Ruth Matiko, Zakaria Mugaya, Sospater Magena, Jackison Sinda, Edith Bosango, Zakaria Kerambo, Paulo Wankaba, Gabrieli Mwita, Zedekia Ayaga.

**Other missionaries:** Clinton & Maybell Ferster, Mahlon & Mabel Hess, Edith Showalter, Elva Landis, Mary Harnish, Alta Weaver, Mary Metzler, Hedy Nacht, Gordon Peters.

**Mara Hills School:** Reuben & Ida Horst, Levi & Mary Hurst, Ruth Bauman, Miriam Buckwalter, Chester & Vivian Denlinger, Clara Landis, Martha Lutz, Leroy & Betty Petersheim, Edith Martin, David & Erma Clemens.

## 4. NYAHONGO

**Congregations and first leaders:**

| | | |
|---|---|---|
| 80 Rwang'enyi | 1938 | Zedekia M. Kisare |
| 81 Nyamkonge (Saragire) | 1939 | Erasto G. Okombo |
| 82 Omoche | 1944 | James N. Oyier* |
| 83 Manyanyi | 1945 | Andrea J. Mwabe |
| 84 Busurwa | 1946 | Zephenia K. Migire, Simon N. Ojende* |
| 85 Nyarombo | 1946 | Yohana W. Wang'ombe |
| 86 Kinyenche | 1950 | Stakus N. Wango |
| 87 Mikondo | 1954 | Eliakim N. Obonyo, Zephania K. Migire |
| 88 Sokorabolo | 1958 | Elsafan Okelo |
| 89 Ryagati | 1964 | Benjamin M. Nyatega |
| 90 Burere | 1966 | Suleman C. Seya* |
| 91 Ngasaro | 1967 | Enoka Kawira |
| 92 Nyamisarwa | 1970 | Richard A. Nyalgose |
| 93 Randa | 1971 | Samwel Nchagwa |
| 94 Kyariko | 1978 | Joseph S. Nyakyema |
| 95 Raranya | 1979 | Richard A. Nyalgose |
| 96 Manila | 1981 | Azaria O. Maganya |
| 97 Kirogo | 1982 | Kenedy O. Ohuya |
| 98 Nyamagaro | 1982 | Malaki Kagose |
| 99 Radienya | 1982 | Elfas O. Nyakiriga |
| 100 Lolwe | 1983 | Eliazar N. Saghe |
| 101 Nyabikondo | 1983 | Meshak A. Mashwa |

*Supervised from Shirati until 1979 when formed into a district.*

**Ordained leaders:**

| | |
|---|---|
| Zephania K. & Rusabella Migire | 1955– |
| Dishon M. & Mikali Ngoya | 1955–66, 1977– |
| Misraim O. & Zilipa Nyagwegwe | 1976–83 |
| Lawrence & Esta Makonyu | 1983– |

*Council secretary*: Naftali M. Machira

**Other leaders and elders:** Nathanael Gomba*, Emmanuel Buchore*, Andrea Juma*, Joshua Abuya*, Eliakim N. Obonyo, Dishon O. Otieno, Benson Odeny, Samuel Ogaga, Rosalina Zakaria, Ruth Mayoyo, Paul Kajina, Rafael Suna, Daniel Kangwe, Ambroz Uromi, Mikael Josese, Elfaz Ogigo Nyakiriga, Joash Mangee, Joash O. Kisugo, Lawrence S. Nyalgose, Joash O. Kiango, James Nyakiema*.

## 5. SHIRATI

**Congregations and first leaders:**

| | | |
|---|---|---|
| 130 | Shirati | 1934 Elam Stauffer, John Mosemann |
| 131 | Tobwe | 1939 Zephania K. Migire, Nashon Nyambok |
| 132 | Kirongwe | 1939 Samuel Ngoga* |
| 133 | Nyahera | 1952 Suleman Marere* |
| 134 | Sota | 1955 Mwinjilisti na James Shank |
| 135 | Michire | 1960 Abednego Musilanga |
| 136 | Bubombi | 1965 Jonathan Mabeche |
| 137 | Gibeni | 1970 Joseph Ayoma* |
| 138 | Nyamagongo | 1975 Joash Abuya* |

*From this district originated Kamageta in 1966 and Nyahongo in 1979.*

**Ordained leaders:**

| | |
|---|---|
| Elam & Elizabeth Stauffer | 1934–35, 1939–46 |
| John & Ruth Mosemann | 1934–39 |
| Clinton & Maybell Ferster | 1935,1939, 1946–48 |
| Noah & Muriel Mack | 1939–40, 1947–49 |
| Merle & Sara Eshleman | 1940–54 |

| | |
|---|---|
| James & Ruth Shank | 1946–56 |
| Zedekia & Susana Kisare | 1950–59, 1979– |
| Nashon & Dorka Nyambok | 1950–53, 1960– |
| Lester & Lois Eshleman | 1952–66 |
| Robert & Florence Keener | 1954–58 |
| Zephania K. & Rusabella Migire | 1955–79 |
| Isaya & Priskilla Obiero | 1955–62 |
| Hershey & Norman Leaman | 1960–64 |
| Victor & Viola Dorsch | 1982– |

*Council secretary*: William Mang'ana

**Other leaders and elders:** Yakobo Obado*, Thadayo Makori*, Simeon Otulo*, Yohana Warioba, Ezron Obwombe, Malaki Kisare, Eliphaz Nyang'oro, Elifalet Maguga, Sitakus Wango, Philemon Kawira, Nikanor Dhaje, Samwel Oloko, James Kabaka, Ernest Mato, Priskilla Isaya, Enoka Kawira, Trufena Enoka.

*Special tasks*: Vivian Eby, Nora Snavely,Curvin Buchen, James Shelly, Daniel Wenger, Nevin & Barbara Kraybill, Gerald Miller, Stella Newswanger, Chris & Laverne Peifer, David & Ginette Leinbach, Jere Brubaker, Marlin & Mary Zimmerman, Jeanette Mummau, Tom & Aletha Franz, Janet Gehman, Bonnie Bergey, Shirley Mast, Allen & Sue Detweiler.

*Doctors and nurses*: Lillie Shenk, Elma Hershberger, Edith Showalter, Elva Landis, Mary Harnish, Ruth Miller, Hedwig Nacht, Elsie Cressman, Velma Eshleman, Alta Weaver, Fred & Millie Brenneman, Harold & Miriam Housman, Alice Reber, Anna Martin, Cora Lehman, Dorcas Stoltzfus, Naomi Weaver, Delilah Detweiler, Richard & Ruth Weaver, Leo & Mary Yoder, Glen & Ellin Brubaker, John & Margaret Keiser, Roger & Elaine Unzicker, Robert & Marian Musser, William & Lois Davidson, Esther Mack, Esther Sweigart, Arnold & Laverne Nickel, Ronald & Viola Lowen, Elias & Hubertine Noordman, Stanley & Susan Godshall, Verle Rufenacht, Harold & Esther Kraybill, Klinton Nyamuryekung'e, Gavyole, Terence & Marilyn Chute, Raymond & Eleanor Martens, Joyce Witmer, Josiah & Esther Kawira.

*Kilimanjaro Christian Medical Center*: Nevin & Barbara Kraybill, Lester & Lois Eshleman, Walter & Mae Schlabach.

*Ilembula Lutheran Hospital*: David & Florence Harnish.

## 6. TARIME

Congregations and first leaders:

| | | | |
|---|---|---|---|
| 160 | Mtana (Bukenye) | 1949 | Nathanael Rhobi |
| 161 | Tarime | 1953 | Nashon Nyambok |
| 162 | Nyabirongo (Bunjari) | 1955 | Gideon Mwita |
| 163 | Kembwe | 1974 | Musa Yakobo |
| 164 | Kiogera | 1983 | Amos Turuka |

*Looked after from Nyabasi until 1966 when constituted as Tarime District. In August 1983 eight congregations were formed into Mori District.*

Ordained leaders and evangelists:

| | |
|---|---|
| Nashon & Dorka Nyambok | 1953–59 |
| Narkiso & Peris Odhiambo | 1959–65 |
| Nathanael & Damari Tingayi | 1965–67 |
| Naftali & Elizabeth Birai | 1967 |
| Salmon & Lois Buteng'e | 1968–70 |
| Gershon & Debora Nyarusanda | 1970–72, 1977– |
| Manaen & Kezia Wadugu | 1972–77 |

*Council secretary*: Jackson Nyangi Mkono

Other leaders and elders: Daudi Kerario, Ruth Wambura, Elisheba Daniel.

## B. Southern Diocese, by districts

### 1. ARUSHA

300 Arusha established 1976 by Daniel Sigira

Ordained leaders:

| | |
|---|---|
| Daniel M. & Susana Sigira | 1976–79 |
| Lester & Lois Eshleman | 1979– |
| Daudi & Dorka Mahemba | 1979–82 |
| Ebanda K. & Magdalena Marukwa | 1982– |

*Council secretary*: Esta Sabuni

Elders: Shadrack Sentchu, Ruth William, Wilson Obure, Stephen Mang'ana, Dorka Mahemba, Stanislaus Nyasibora, Silas Nyanyika, Charles Abuya, E.D.Nyasibora, Manaen Kawira.

### 2. BIHARAMULO

Congregations and first leaders:

| | | | |
|---|---|---|---|
| 310 | Ichwankima | 1970 | J. Wera Magangira, Ebanda K. Marukwa |
| 311 | Chato | 1973 | Ebanda K. Marukwa |
| 312 | Mwangaza | 1981 | Joakim Joel |
| 313 | Busarara | 1983 | Salmon Nyamugundu |

Evangelists and ordained leaders:

| | |
|---|---|
| Jackson Wera & Monika Magangira | 1970–75 |
| Ebanda K. & Magdalena Marukwa | 1970–80 |
| Salmon Musikwa & Juliana Nyamugundu | 1981– |

*Council secretary*: Elias Nyasonga

Other leaders and elders: Hezekia Masora, Elias Karebe, Dina Antoni, Lukas Morera, Livingstone Rusaka, Joakim Joel, Christopher Mikaeli, Edmon Zakayo, J. B. Kasonde.

### 3. BUKIROBA

Congregations and first leaders:

| | | | |
|---|---|---|---|
| 340 | Nyabange | 1935 | Elam Stauffer |
| 341 | Bisumwa (Kyenyiboko, Nyabikwabi) | 1946 | Nyerere Itinde |
| 342 | Nyankanga | 1953 | Petro Makondo*, Gabriel Kituhu* |
| 343 | Kiagata | 1958 | Salmon Nyamugundu, George Smoker |

Ordained leaders:

| | |
|---|---|
| Elam & Elizabeth Stauffer | 1935–36, 1947–48 |

| | |
|---|---|
| John & Catharine Leatherman | 1936–49, 1952–65 |
| Eby & Elva Leaman | 1939–43 |
| George & Dorothy Smoker | 1939–70 |
| Levi & Mary Hurst | 1948–52 |
| Elam & Grace Stauffer | 1949–50 |
| Clyde & Alta Shenk | 1950–51, 1966–68 |
| Donald & Anna Ruth Jacobs | 1959–66 |
| Robert & Florence Keener | 1959–63 |
| Joseph & Edith Shenk | 1966–76 |
| Zedekia & Susana Kisare | 1966–79 |
| Nashon N. & Naomi Nyambalya | 1966–71 |
| Naftali & Elizabeth Birai | 1970–80 |
| Daudi & Dorka Mahemba | 1971–74 |
| Victor & Viola Dorsch | 1971–77 |
| Daniel & Erma Wenger | 1976–79, 1982–83 |
| Joseph & Gloria Bontrager | 1977–82 |
| Salmon Musikwa & Juliana Nyamugundu | 1980–81 |
| Daniel Imori & Rhoda Mtoka | 1981– |

*Council secretary*: Elifaz S.Matera

**Other leaders and elders**: Timoteo na Mariamu Magoti*, Daniel Opanga, Yakobo Wambura, Samson Kigoya*, Ludia Waibe*, Priska Nyabweke, Koren Togoro, Esta Nyangi, John Onyango, Salmon Nkonyi, Pius Nyangi, Eliafaz S. Matera, Perucy Kyambirya, Samson Kondoro, Eliasafu M. Saira.

**Other missionaries**: Clinton & Maybell Ferster, Noah & Muriel Mack, Grace Metzler, Phebe Yoder, Velma Eshleman, Miriam Wenger, Stella Newswanger, Ken Brunk, Don & Judy Stoltzfus, Robert & Betty Lou Buckwalter, Mahlon & Mabel Hess, Simeon & Edna Hurst, Eugene & Hazel Frey.

*Katoke Teacher Training Center*: Donald & Anna Ruth Jacobs, Maynard Kurtz, Laura Kurtz

*Morembe School*: Rhoda Wenger, Grace Gehman, Laura Kurtz

*YMCA Farm School (Moshi)*: Jerry & Sharon Stutzman

*Accountants, secretaries*: Rhoda Hess, Naomi Smoker, Vivian Eby, Nyerere Itinde, Martha Myer, Arlene Garber, Evelyn Atkinson, Elaine Breckbill, Ruth Ann Sensenig.

*Artisans*: Sam & Esther Freed Troyer, John & Bertha Graybill, Ivan Sell, James & Martha Mohler, Dale & Dorka Ressler.

## 4. BUMANGI

**Congregations and first leaders**:

| | | |
|---|---|---|
| 370 Bumangi | 1937 | Clyde Shenk |
| 371 Masurura | 1945 | Zakaria M. Mahuka |
| 372 Butiama | 1949 | Mishael Kanyasi |
| 373 Bisarye | 1951 | Thomas Simba |
| 374 Ryamugabo | 1951 | Jona Itine Mirari* |
| 375 Mugeta | 1953 | Thomas Tumbo, Ndugu Sulemani |
| 376 Nyamuswa | 1954 | Mwl. Alexander, Thomas Simba |
| 377 Nyamika | 1957 | Jona I. Mirari* |
| 378 Nyangiri | 1958 | Amon Maseba |
| 379 Kyabakari | 1957 | Daniel Sigira, Eliya Wandiba |
| 380 Murunguta | 1962 | Robati Mguzu |
| 381 Rwamukoma | 1963 | Elisha N. Meso |
| 382 Kihumbu | 1963 | Elisha N. Meso |
| 383 Nyamikoma | 1963 | Jackisoni Matayi |
| 384 Kamugege | 1963 | Eliya Wandiba |
| 385 Sarawe | 1964 | Stefano I. Tingayi |
| 386 Salama (Kironero) | 1964 | Jackisoni Matayi |
| 387 Rwamakore | 1965 | Jonathan R. Magesa* |
| 388 Tarani | 1966 | Jackisoni Mtika |
| 389 Kibubwa | 1966 | Lazaro Kibeyo |
| 390 Muryaza | 1981 | Erasto Nyamusika |
| 391 Kizaru | 1981 | Mwikwabi Serikali |

**Ordained leaders**:

| | |
|---|---|
| J. Clyde & Alta Shenk | 1936–50 |
| Clinton & Maybell Ferster | 1937, 1945–46 |
| Mahlon & Mabel Hess | 1946–47, 1954–62 |
| Elam & Grace Stauffer | 1950–52 |
| Donald & Anna Ruth Jacobs | 1954–56 |
| Jona I* & Lea Mirari | 1956–70 |

159

Elisha N. & Susana Meso 1956–
Eliya & Muzubi Wandiba 1976–
Erasto M. & Silibia Nyamusika 1979–

**Council secretary**: Jackisoni Matayi

**Other leaders and elders**: Samson Nyanduga*, Yohana Mzarari*, Nashon Waryoba*, Ezra Sungura*, Mishail Muboga*, Amosi Waryoba*, Joshua Rubirya*, Edwadi Fekaikisamo, Sospita W. Sasaba, Stephano Masima, Wambura Skuri, Yohana Rugoye, Herman Kataraia, Phinehas Nyang'oro, Kembo Migire*, Sospeter Muttani.

**Other missionaries**: Rhoda Wenger, Vivian Eby, Elam & Elizabeth Stauffer, John & Catharine Leatherman, James & Ruth Shank, Robert & Florence Keener, Ken Brunk, Don Stoltzfus, Daniel Maxwell, Mark Day.

## 5. BUNDA (Majita B)

**Congregations and first leaders**:

| | | |
|---|---|---|
| 410 Nyambono | 1944 | Lameki Maiba, Mishael Kanyasi |
| 411 Masinono | 1948 | Musa Adongo |
| 412 Saragana | 1949 | Eliazari M. Mkama |
| 413 Wanyere | 1951 | Zakaria Mwendwa Machumu, Muttani Maragwa |
| 414 Chirorwe | 1952 | James Ndege Nengo, James M.Busanya, |
| 415 Bugoji | 1954 | Donaldi Kabaja, Gershon Nyarusanda |
| 416 Kaburabura | 1957 | Timotheo M. Buruge, Eliakim Kuboja |
| 417 Kabasa | 1961 | Hezekia N.Sarya, Paulo M. Mauma |
| 418 Kabainja | 1963 | Elikana Nyanjeo, Elias Kasanga |
| 419 Mcharo | 1963 | Thomas Simba, Amosi Mwita |
| 420 Kamukenga | 1965 | Joramu Tanda, Ebanda K. Marukwa |
| 421 Bunda | 1965 | Naftali Joliga, Adonias Chibunu |
| 422 Mwisenyi | 1965 | Lameck J. Karuguru |
| 423 Nyamitwebiri | 1965 | Mashauri Nyambele |
| 424 Kung'ombe | 1970 | Joktani Kasara |
| 425 Mirambi | 1974 | Yakobo Hunghu |
| 426 Manara | 1974 | Petro Masanja |
| 427 Guta | 1982 | Aristablo M. Wanjara |

*Supervised from Mugano until 1960 and from Majita until 1971 when established as a district.*

**Ordained leaders**:

| | |
|---|---|
| Hezekia & Perusi Sarya | 1960–69 |
| Musa Adongo & Helena Abura | 1960–74 |
| Daniel & Susana Sigira | 1971–76, 1979–82 |
| Japhet M. & Rebeka Maiga | 1975– |
| Sospeter & Kezia Muttani | 1981– |
| Mishael M.& Penina Nyasonga | 1983– |
| Phares K. & Tabu Sasumwa | 1983– |
| Petro & Agnes Masanja | 1983– |

**Council secretary**: Mishael Nyasonga

**Other leaders and elders**: Kristopher O. Kulembwa*, Daudi Kagondo, Naomi Bunyinyiga, Andrea N. Magesa, Stephano M. Ndaro, Donald N. Muso, Jackson M. Majagwa, Josephat M. Mabeba, Eliakimu K. Magenda, Andrea Mashole, Kezia Marinjaga, Phinias Rukondo, Joshua M. Mujungu, Elias K.Kasanga, Lazaro Misungwi, Zaburoni Ndoroba, Salimoni Mabega, Ndugu Mgongo, Joseph Rumbika.

## 6. DAR ES SALAAM

**Congregations and first leaders**:

| | | | |
|---|---|---|---|
| 450 | Kibasila | 1963 | Mahlon Hess |
| 451 | Mnazi Mrefu, Ukonga | 1982 | John Nyagwegwe |

**Ordained leaders**:

| | |
|---|---|
| Mahlon & Mabel Hess | 1963–65 |
| Daudi & Dorka Mahemba | 1964–71 |
| Hezekia & Perusi Sarya | 1971–79 |
| Phinehas & Penina Nyang'oro | 1976–79 |
| Ebanda K. & Magdalena Marukwa | 1980–82 |
| Daniel Mato & Susana Sigira | 1982– |

*Council secretary*: Miriam Dhudha

**Elders**: William Matangara*, Daniel Mahemba, Kembo Migire*, Phares Bwana*, Joseph Butiku, Laura Kurtz, John Mkula, Zakayo Maswera, Jackson Nyakirangani, James Nyakyoma, Naftali Obiero, Stefano Bituro, Esta Joseph, Jessica Makindi, Christina Nyagiro, Jonathan Magwega, Samuel Kisare, Josiah Muganda.

**Other missionaries**: Ray Martin, Allen Busenitz, Harold & Annetta Miller, Charles Bauman, Eric & Fran Schiller.

## 7. DODOMA

460 Dodoma established 1983 by K. J. Kaema, evangelist.

### Ordained leaders:

Phinehas & Penina Nyang'oro        1979–
S. Majinge & Christiana Karuguru    1981–83

*Council secretary*: Eleazari Majani Busanga

**Elders**: Edward Karuguru, James & Esther Olimo, Nashon Nyambita, Perusi Ntangwa.

## 8. KISAKA

### Congregations and first leaders:

| | | |
|---|---|---|
| 470 Kisaka | 1954 | Clyde Shenk |
| 471 Busawe | 1958 | Boaz Naam |
| 472 Kenyana | 1960 | Naaman Agola |
| 473 Rung'abure (Nyamemba) | 1963 | Yakobo Chacha* |
| 474 Masinki | 1963 | Samuel Kitano* |
| 475 Buchanchari | 1967 | Jackson Nyambabe*, Elisha Makaiga* |

### Ordained leaders:

J. Clyde & Alta Shenk            1954–65
Daniel & Susana Sigira          1964–71
Nashon & Naomi Nyambalya    1971–
Jackson* & Rebeka Nyambabe    1976–80

*Council secretary*: ⸺⸺⸺

**Other leaders and elders**: Zedekia Kisare, Joash Lore*, Josefu Nyamuhanga Musimbiti*, Elisha N. Meso, Eliya M. Wandiba, Samuel Nyarukoba*, Elifaz Odundo, Daniel Osewe, Nathanael Odera, Ezron Maswe, Ludia Mukami, Terezia Richard, Caleb Randa, Kainda Matunia, Wilkista Juma, Elisha Makarara, Daudi Kirangi, Reuben Aganyo.

**Other missionaries**: Velma Eshleman, Mary Harnish.

## 9. MAJITA (Majita A)

### Congregations and first leaders:

| | | |
|---|---|---|
| 500 Rwanga | 1929 | Petro M. Mangaru, Tito Chinuno |
| 501 Busekera | 1933 | Thomas Chasa |
| 502 Bwenda (Nyamulibwa, Rwamatoke) | 1933 | Mikael Nyachiriga Naftali M. Mugenyi James Busanya |
| 503 Kwikerege | 1933 | Paulo Chai Chemere |
| 504 Buringa | 1933 | Saulo Kumira |
| 505 Butata | 1934 | Mutumwa Kasereka, Ibrahimu Ryahaha |
| 506 Bugunda | 1936 | Gugai Bundara, Thomas Rukondo |
| 507 Bukima | 1936 | Majara Chigoye |
| 508 Musanja | 1939 | Zakaria Mabuba |
| 509 Kanyega (Mrangi) | 1941 | Stephano Magarya, Ndugu Biraso, John Muyabi, Masamaga Changuru |
| 510 Nyang'ombe | 1944 | Naaman K. Kujerwa |
| 511 Seka | 1949 | Samson M. Masija |
| 512 Nyambui | 1961 | Naftali Joliga |
| 513 Karusenyi | 1962 | Shadrack M. Nyachirenge |
| 514 Chakaroso | 1964 | Berias M. Magoma |
| 515 Chitare | 1964 | Gidioni R. Majabe, Misana Maguguli |
| 516 Chimati | 1966 | Josephati M. Manyama |
| 517 Kome | 1974 | Nashon Magembe, Venaus M. Magere |
| 518 Stooni (Gurio) | 1974 | Aristarko Masese, Phinehas Kende |
| 519 Bwasi | 1974 | Andrea R. Chemere |
| 520 Chumwi | 1975 | Zaburoni K. Nyasore |

521 Busungu 1976 Reuben Sumuni
522 Ryasembe 1978 Adoram M.
Manyama
523 Mabuimerafuru 1983 Sosthene W. Marija
524 Buira 1983 Venaus M. Chikara

*Oversight from Mugango until 1960 when
established as Majita District. In 1971 the
appropriate congregations were formed into
Bunda District.*

**Ordained leaders:**

| | |
|---|---|
| Andrea & Rebeka Mabeba | 1950–61 |
| Paulo & Marta Chemere | 1955– |
| Aristarko & Perusi Masese | 1960– |
| Naftali Magai & Kezia Mugenyi | 1982– |
| Naaman Kubebeka & | |
| Susana Kujerwa | 1982– |
| Elias Magabiro & Zilipa Magoro | 1982– |

***Council secretary:*** Charles Makene Mulebo

**Other leaders and elders:** Ezekieli Mganga,
Eliabu Musiba Bundara, Azaria Misana Bwire,
Stefano Magarya, Paulo Musyangi Mauma,
Daniel M. Sigira, Daniel Maungo, Yohana
Sagaya, Reuben Mangunu, Rudara Kusyama,
Nashoni Chiganga Abusero*, Gideon Muga,
Zakaria Masanga Sokoro, Joel Sakire, Joel
Malembela, Yakobo Songoma, James Maingu
Musumi, Paulo Musa, Yohana Chikubure,
Sirasi Nyamhura, Yohana Mberege, Samson
Kerenge, Stefano Kusaga, Nyamwoya
Ngereja, Musa Makene Mulebo, Haruni
Kamara, Thomas Mujuberi, Hosea Buremo,
Loisi Nyarugera, Elizabeti Nyamasokoro,
Efraim Chitana* & Mariamu Maganda,
Josefati Mfuati*, Ananias Nyajoro*, Stefano
Magarya*, Arfured Magoti, Timotheo Makoje,
Paulo Mwenura, Stefano Sumuni, Zabron
Kuyenga, Petro Malyango, Timotheo Muniji,
William Mafworo, Joseph Kuyenga*,
Parapara Mutaju*, Jackson Kajeri, Eliasafu
Murimbo, Eliakim Mapesi Magoti, Ezra
Butiku, Gershon M. Nyarusanda, Jemima
Chitana, Jackson Jengo, Zakayo Maswera,
Petro Nyamhura, Andrea Masaru, Androniko
Magoti, Naftali Matome, Stanislaus & Eunike
Nyamanda, Mikael Matara Kaema, Josephat

Mwagara, Fredirick Mangunu, Julius Bulemo,
K. J. Kaema, Jackson Mingu, Damari Kamoga
Makene, Ezekieli Mafuru.

## 10. MUGANGO

**Congregations and first leaders:**

| | | | |
|---|---|---|---|
| 550 | Busumi | 1932 | Silas Mayega |
| 551 | Mugango | 1936 | Elam Stauffer |
| 552 | Maneke | 1944 | Yohana Sagaya |
| | (Rutare, | | |
| | Busambara) | | |
| 553 | Tegeruka | 1948 | Hezekia N. Sarya |
| 554 | Nyakatende | 1950 | Daniel M. Sigira |
| 555 | Mayani | 1957 | Elisha Omeri |
| | (Katario) | | |
| 556 | Kiriba | 1960 | Reguregu Musiba |
| 557 | Mwiringo | 1974 | Naftali M. Kagumu |
| 558 | Bwai | 1982 | Samwel Katama |

*Majita-Bunda congregations established as new
district in 1960.*

**Ordained leaders:**

| | |
|---|---|
| Elam & Elizabeth Stauffer | 1936–38 |
| Ray & Miriam Wenger | 1938–45, |
| Miriam | 1949–54 |
| Levi & Mary Hurst | 1945–48 |
| Mahlon & Mabel Hess | 1948–50, |
| | 1952–54 |
| Ezekiel & Raheri Muganda | 1950–54 |
| Elam & Grace Stauffer | 1954–59 |
| Daniel & Susana Sigira | 1956–64 |
| Andrea & Rebeka Mabeba | 1961–81 |
| Isaya & Lusia Onyango | 1979– |
| Daudi & Dorka Mahemba | 1982– |

***Council secretary:*** Isaya A. Onyango

**Other leaders and elders:** Petro Makongoro
Mangaru, Simeon Magoti Sanjaga, Paulo Chai
Chemere, Naftali Magai Mugenyi, Gideon
Magesa Muga, Mishael Masatu Kanyasi,
Ndege Simeon*, Josaphati Majinge, Joshua
Nyachimogoro, Naftali Kagumu, Daudi
Osoya, Stefano Onyango, Nashon Okech,
James Busanya, Zedekea Magafu*, Yeremia
Bukuyu*, Yusuf Majura, Stefano Magarya,
Elia Rumbika Maseme, Thomas Nyambere,

Thomas Maginga*, Stefano Chibure, Ndugu Nyakuringa(Maneke), Nikodemu Meli Nyamageu, Jackson Biraso.

**Other missionaries**: Clinton & Maybell Ferster, Phebe Yoder, Rhoda Wenger, Elma Hershberger, Vivian Eby, John & Catharine Leatherman, Clyde & Alta Shenk, Hedy Nacht, Mary Metzler, Laura Kurtz.

## 11. MUSOMA

### Congregations and first leaders:

| | | | |
|---|---|---|---|
| 580 | Musoma | 1937 | Elam Stauffer, John Leatherman, Daniel Opanga |
| 581 | Nyarusurya | 1966 | Gideon M. Nyasebwa |
| 582 | Mkirira | 1970 | Nashon Muttani |

*Musoma Congregation overseen from Bukiroba until 1954.*

### Ordained leaders:

| | |
|---|---|
| Ezekiel K. & Raheri Muganda | 1954–74 |
| Elam & Grace Stauffer | 1959–64 |
| Clyde & Alta Shenk | 1964–65 |
| Daudi W. & Dorka Mahemba | 1974–79 |
| Erasto & Silibia Nyamusika | 1979–81 |
| Eliasafu & Rachel Igira | 1981–82 |
| Nathanael & Damari Tingayi | 1982– |

*Council secretary*: Shadrack Mwiyare

**Other leaders and elders**: Nathanael Rhobi Nyamare, Daniel Opanga, Ezekieli Galikika, Rafael Faru, A. M. Chirangi, D. Keregero, Samuel Adongo, Daniel Mahemba, Haruni Sabaganya, Susana Agola, Rhoda William, Esther Olimo, Rhoda Mahemba, William Magolanga, Thomas Kahinda, Sara Nashon, Gideon Muga, Charles Mukakaro, Daniel Sattima, Eliasafu Samanyi, Magret Ismael, Nathan Waiga Agai.

**Other missionaries**: Leroy & Betty Petersheim.

***Musoma Alliance Secondary School***: Mark Brubaker, Donald Mellinger, Maynard & Hilda Kurtz, Joseph & Edith Shenk, Robert & Florence Keener, Lewis & Ann Naylor, Ernest & Lois Hess, Omar & Anna Kathryn Eby, Allen & Marabeth Busenitz, Rhoda Wenger (also Ashira), Laura Kurtz.

## 12. MWANZA

590 Mwanza established 1970 by Naftali Birai from Musoma.

### Ordained leaders:

| | |
|---|---|
| Jona I.* & Lea Mirari | 1970–76 |
| Salmon S. & Lois Buteng'e | 1976–81 |
| Julius & Zena Bulemo | 1981– |

*Council secretary*: Josephat Omuyanja

**Elders**: Willison Masiaga*, Samson Nyanduga*, Deus Wanjara, Lameck Sakire, Naaman Ademba, Rebeka Ademba, Samueli Kitati, Samueli Misana, Meshak Merengo, Rebeka Nyakiha, Boniphace Tairo

## 13. ROGORO (Ikoma/Mugumu)

### Congregations and first leaders:

| | | | |
|---|---|---|---|
| 600 | Robanda | 1949 | Daudi Mahemba |
| 601 | Morotonga | 1956 | Petro Makondo* |
| 602 | Issenye, Nagusi | 1959 | Gershon Ayoo Mbudi |
| 603 | Miseke | 1963 | Samson Kiroto, Churchill Mwikwabe |
| 604 | Nyichoka | 1967 | Elia Goshashi |
| 605 | Rwamchanga | 1967 | Wilson Gimongi* |
| 606 | Mugumu | 1968 | Efraim Mbota* |
| 607 | Kisangura | 1969 | Kanisa la Friends |
| 608 | Bwitengi | 1970 | Petro Makondo* |
| 609 | Burunga | 1974 | Samson Kiberiti |
| 610 | Itununu | 1978 | Damari Nyangi |

*Council secretary*: Paulo Shanyangi

*Others giving pastoral care were Clyde Shenk, John Leatherman, George & Dorothy Smoker and Joseph Shenk (in early years; while no resident pastor).*

**Ordained leaders:**

| | |
|---|---|
| Daudi W. & Dorka Mahemba | 1961–64 |
| Marko Kisigiro* | 1972–81 |
| Victor & Viola Dorsch | 1977–81 |
| Salmon S. & Lois Buteng'e | 1981– |

*Council secretary*: Paulo Shanyangi

**Other leaders and elders:** Philemon Mbota, Paulo Muhando, Sara Magesa, Ezra Butiku, Leonard Kubebeka, Saimon Kabati, Alexander Makorere, Wilson Machota, Mariamu* Kisigiro, Paulo Muhere, Christopher Ndori, Martin Yusufu, Shadrack Magolina, Stefano Karumanga, Christopher M. Ndege.

**Other missionaries:** Albert & Annie Drudge, Thomas & Jill Miller.

### 14. TABORA

630 Tabora established 1976 by J. Wera Magangira; services held at Kitete until leader transferred in 1980. Reopened 1983 in Molangidu village.

**Ordained leader:**

Jackson Wera & Monika Magangira    1981–

*Secretary-evangelist*: Andrea Kilori

**Elders:** Shingwa Jinara, Machiya Jinara, Lufunga Ndulila, Charles Manzalima, Elias Limbu.

## C. BISHOPS AND OFFICERS

### 1. Tanganyika Mennonite Church Kanisa la Mennonite Tanzania

**BISHOPS:**

| | |
|---|---|
| Elam W. Stauffer | 1938–64 |
| Ray W. Wenger | 1941–45 |
| Simeon W. Hurst | 1955–64 |
| Donald R. Jacobs | 1964–66 |
| Zedekia M. Kisare | 1966– |
| Hezekia N. Sarya | 1977– |

**OFFICERS:**
  **Chairman:**

| | |
|---|---|
| Elam W. Stauffer | 1960–62, 64 |
| Zedekia M. Kisare | 1963, 1967–80 |
| Donald R. Jacobs | 1965–66 |

  **Asst. Chairman:**

| | |
|---|---|
| Simeon W. Hurst | 1960–62, 64 |
| Ezekiel K. Muganda | 1963, 1967–73 |
| Zedekia M. Kisare | 1965–66 |
| Hezekia N. Sarya | 1974–80 |

  **Secretary:**

| | |
|---|---|
| John E. Leatherman | 1960–61 |
| Kembo Migire* | 1962 |
| Eliam M. Mauma* | 1963–69 |
| A. Mutaragara Chirangi | 1970–80 |

  **Asst. Secretary:**

| | |
|---|---|
| Kembo Migire* | 1963 |
| Donald R. Jacobs | 1964 |
| J. Clyde Shenk | 1965–69 |
| Naftali M. Birai | 1970–74 |
| Joseph C. Shenk | 1975–77 |
| Salmon S. Butenge | 1978–80 |

  **Treasurer:**

| | |
|---|---|
| Elisha N. Meso | 1962–67 |
| Nyerere W. Itinde | 1967–70 |
| Salmon S. Butenge | 1971–75 |
| Naftali M. Birai | 1976–80 |

### 2. North Mara Diocese:

  **Chairman:**

| | |
|---|---|
| Zedekia M. Kisare | 1980– |

  **Asst. Chairman:**

| | |
|---|---|
| Nashon K. Nyambok | 1980– |

  **Secretary-Treasurer:**

| | |
|---|---|
| Naftali M. Birai | 1980– |

### 3. Southern Diocese:

  **Chairman:**

| | |
|---|---|
| Hezekia N. Sarya | 1980– |

  **Asst. Chairman:**

| | |
|---|---|
| Aristarko M. Masese | 1980–82 |
| Salmon S. Buteng'e | 1982– |

  **Secretary:**

| | |
|---|---|
| Elisha N. Meso | 1980–82 |
| Daniel I. Mtoka | 1982– |

  **Treasurer:**

| | |
|---|---|
| Salmon S. Buteng'e | 1980–82 |
| Eliasafu M. Igira | 1982– |

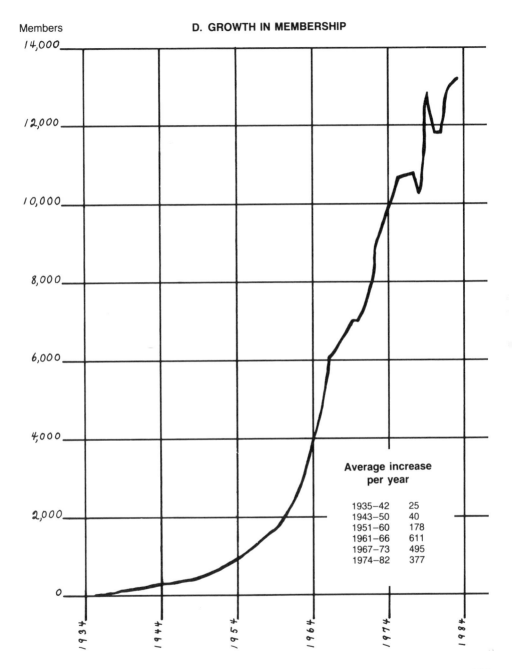

**D. GROWTH IN MEMBERSHIP**

Members

14,000

12,000

10,000

8,000

6,000

4,000

2,000

0

Average increase
per year

| | |
|---|---|
| 1935–42 | 25 |
| 1943–50 | 40 |
| 1951–60 | 178 |
| 1961–66 | 611 |
| 1967–73 | 495 |
| 1974–82 | 377 |

1934  1944  1954  1964  1974  1984

## E. MEMBERSHIP AND OFFERINGS 1982

### North Mara Diocese

|  | Congregations | Members | Offerings |
|---|---|---|---|
| 1. Kamageta | 12 | 480 | shs  5,786 |
| 2. Mori[1] | — | — | — |
| 3. Nyabasi | 12 | 580 | 24,054 |
| 4. Nyahongo | 22 | 1,149 | 11,349 |
| 5. Shirati | 8 | 1,028 | 27,230 |
| 6. Tarime[2] | 13 | 693 | 25,065 |
|  | 67 | 3,930[3] | shs 93,484 |

### Southern Diocese

|  | Congregations | Members | Offerings |
|---|---|---|---|
| 1. Arusha | 1 | 53 | shs 10,224 |
| 2. Biharamulo | 4 | 108 | 958 |
| 3. Bukiroba | 4 | 700 | 22,101 |
| 4. Bumangi | 22 | 1,080 | 10,000 |
| 5. Bunda | 18 | 2,577 | 26,600 |
| 6. Dar es Salaam | 2 | 170 | 46,559 |
| 7. Dodoma[4] | 1 | — | — |
| 8. Kisaka | 6 | 518 | 5,988 |
| 9. Majita | 25 | 2,797 | 54,853 |
| 10. Mugango | 9 | 782 | 12,647 |
| 11. Musoma | 3 | 286 | 12,450 |
| 12. Mwanza | 1 | 174 | 25,534 |
| 13. Rogoro | 11 | 248 | 22,258 |
| 14. Tabora[5] | 1 | 7 | — |
|  | 108 | 9,500[6] | shs 250,172 |
| Grand Total | 175 | 13,430 | shs 343,656 |

**Explanatory notes:**
1 In August 1983 Mori District was formed out of Tarime District, constituted of 8 congregations and 450 members. For 1982 their membershp and offerings are included in the Tarime statistics.
2 This step left Tarime District with 5 congregations and 250 members.
3 The report in *Mennonite Yearbook* shows 4,181 members. It would appear that backsliders and transfers were deleted in preparing these statistics.
4 Established in 1983 with 83 members.
5 The congregation was inactive in 1982.
6 *Mennonite Yearbook* shows 8,769 members. It would appear that for this report some districts gave membership figures as of June 1983.

# F. SCHOOLS ESTABLISHED BY TMC

## Primary schools

| | | | | | |
|---|---|---|---|---|---|
| 1. | Mugango | 1947 | 19. | Mangucha | 1956 |
| 2. | Mkoma | 1948 | 20. | Masinono | 1956 |
| 3. | Mrangi | 1948 | 21. | Musanja | 1956 |
| 4. | Kyasamiti | 1951 | 22. | Nyahera | 1956 |
| 5. | Nyabange | 1951 | 23. | Nyakunguru | 1956 |
| 6. | Nyarero | 1952 | 24. | Omoche | 1956 |
| 7. | Nyakatende | 1952 | 25. | Robanda | 1956 |
| 8. | Nyahongo | 1953 | 26. | Kwikerege | 1963 |
| 9. | Kirongwe | 1954 | 27. | Kabasa | 1964 |
| 10. | Kyoruba | 1954 | 28. | Kenyana | 1964 |
| 11. | Masurura | 1954 | 29. | Kirinero | 1964 |
| 12. | Nyiboko | 1954 | 30. | Kisangura | 1964 |
| 13. | Roche | 1954 | 31. | Rwanga & Kasoma | 1964 |
| 14. | Ryamugabo | 1955 | 32. | Bwenda | 1965 |
| 15. | Wanyere | 1955 | 33. | Chirorwe | 1965 |
| 16. | Azimio,Musoma | 1956 | 34. | Seronera | 1966 |
| 17. | Busekera | 1956 | 35. | Getasamo | 1967 |
| 18. | Busumi | 1956 | | | |

## Boarding schools

| | | | | | |
|---|---|---|---|---|---|
| 1. | Bumangi | 1948 | 3. | Morembe | 1958 |
| 2. | Shirati | 1954 | 4. | Musoma Alliance | 1958 |

# III. FOOTNOTES

**Photo section, "With the Lord":**
Four children lie buried in the small graveyard at Shirati: the Stauffer infant, stillborn in 1935; Daniel Hurst, who lived but a few hours in 1946; and the Clemens children, Valerie Ann 1961-65, and David Randall, 1962-65. Also buried there are Alta Shenk and a young German partner with Karl Lauterbach, sisal grower and ropemaker of the colonial era.

**Chapter 1**
1. This is a condensation and translation of a traditional story recorded by K. J. Kaema, an Mjita evangelist.
2. For this book Bishop Zedekia Kisare updated a part of his message in *Called to Be Sent,* Paul N. Kraybill (editor), pp. 162-3.
3. An African financier, Acts 8:26-40; an Asian religionist, 9:3-19 and 23:1; an Italian military man, 10:1-48.
4. Pioneer missionaries to Africa established the custom that at baptism each person choose a biblical name symbolizing that he is a new person in faith and way of life, a practice that came to be followed by all denominations. Elam Stauffer and others often advised that the names given by parents were completely satisfactory. Only a few persons followed his counsel, such as Nyerere Itinde of Bukiroba and Mwita Mambya of Nyarero, now at Mugumu.
5. Genesis 3:1-24.
6. This segment, as also the free verse at the beginning and end of chapter 10, are a summation by the author of his understanding of the biblical message in the light of church history; it is a theological statement of his theme, the pilgrimage of faith. Some of these insights were picked up from Tanzanian preachers and others were inspired by Leslie Newbigin's *The Open Secret* (Grand Rapids, Mich., 1978).

**Chapter 2**
1. It is reported that Roman Catholics came to Majita in 1885, teachers in a school to train clerks and messengers for the colonial government. Ezekiel Muganda's father and uncles, members of the chiefly clan, were among those compelled by whip to attend the school.
2. In this chapter, "Mennonites of North America" refers to the denomination known as *Mennonite Church.* Our brothers of the *General Conference Mennonite Church* and of the *Mennonite Brethren* came in other migrations.
3. Anabaptists trace their origins to Conrad Grebel, Felix Manz, George Blaurock and fellow believers who baptized one another in a prayer meeting in Zurich, Switzerland, on January 21,

1525. Later Menno Simons, a Frisian from the Netherlands, became their chief leader. While they built upon the work of Luther and Zwingli, Anabaptist tenets regarding believer's baptism, voluntary church membership, life of discipleship, and love for enemies were distinctive.

a. The Scriptures are the final guide for faith and practice.
b. The Holy Spirit leads the gathered congregation in discerning the will of God.
c. Believers walk as Jesus walked, bearing the cross after him in self-giving love.
d. Out of love for all men they are willing to lay down life; they do not use the sword nor ask for its protection.
e. Baptism is for those who have trusted Christ and committed themselves to the brotherhood, Christ's body; the church is loyal to Christ alone and membership is voluntary.
f. Through brotherly admonition believers take moral responsibility one for another.
g. Worldly goods are a stewardship, to be shared with brothers and sisters and anyone in need. (Cornelius J. Dyck (ed.), *An Introduction to Mennonite History*, pp. 103-7.)

4. Many of these evangelists also promoted missions. In his evangelistic efforts Noah H. Mack ministered to Phebe Yoder's congregation in Kansas. Mack, a missionary to the blacks of the Welsh Mountain, New Holland, Pa., became one of the bishop counselors for the Tanzania missionaries. Dr. Noah Mack was a near relative. John W. Weaver, a charter member of EMBMC, was the grandfather of Dr. Richard Weaver. A. D. Wenger, second president of Eastern Mennonite College, was the father of Rhoda Wenger.

## Chapter 3

1. This building is still in use. After twenty years as a dispensary, it was enlarged to become a kitchen-dining room for the unmarried missionaries. Currently it provides office and guest facilities for Shirati District churches. A stone commemorating the 50th anniversary was placed on this building.

2. Ibrahim's wife accompanied him to church for a time. While she later discontinued, she no longer hindered him. Ibrahim persevered in his pilgrimage of faith for nearly forty years when the Lord called him home.

3. After he was married and had a family of children, Jona fell into sin. He repented and was reassigned as an evangelist, and in 1956 was called as a pastor and served fourteen years. Then he backslid again. There are those who are continuing to pray for him, and God is continuing to deal with him. However, those women who invoked a curse upon Jona, Clyde, and Alta, have long since died.

## Chapter 4

1. This brother found spiritual healing, and his home church restored him to the pastoral ministry. He served more than twenty years until the Lord called him home.

## Chapter 5

1. Since East African revival began in Burundi and Uganda, the revival song is often sung in Luganda; its chorus begins "Tukutendereza, Yesu," *We praise you, Jesus,* picked up from the song of the Uganda martyrs.

2. 1 John 1:5-10.

3. In 1952 the colonial government recognized Doctor Mack for outstanding medical ministries, awarding him the citation, O.B.E. (Officer of the British Empire).

4. This alliance, LMEC, strengthened and coordinated the educational programs of the missions. After the churches came to autonomy, they continued the alliance as Lake Churches Education Council. After government assumed full responsibility for national education, the council was dissolved. Its original goals had been attained, except the establishment of an AIM school.

5. Because *Spiritual Songs* included favorite revival hymns and was available at a low price, it has enjoyed a large circulation. By 1983, 200,000 copies had been printed and sold.

6. The Lutherans fulfilled the commitments made to the local people. They used the stones John Leatherman had gathered for one of their buildings; they refer to its "Mennonite foundation."

## Chapter 6

1. Shirati is one of thirteen hospitals in the KCMC flying-doctor circuits. Lester consults with Shirati and Mugumu doctors by radiophone weekly, and visits them a number of times each year.

## Chapter 7

1. Mennonite Theological College was administered by Joseph Shenk for a period beginning in 1967.

2. Administrators who followed were Nevin Kraybill (two separate terms), Matiku Nyitambe, Naftali Birai, Manaen Kawira, and Benjamin Migire.

3. By 1983, 330 nurses had graduated from the Shirati Nurses and Midwives Training Center.

## Chapter 8

1. One observer commented: "The church never recovered from the loss of its schools." Across the nation, few denominations or congregations responded to the new challenges.

2. After one year Alta Shenk died in a plane crash. Clyde married Miriam Wenger in 1970, and they carried forward the Kenya ministries. In 1976 Nashon Arwa was ordained to oversee the Migori area and Musa Adongo for the Songor area. (Adongo and his family had returned from Masinono, Musoma, Tanzania, where he had served as a deacon.)

At the end of 1976, Clyde and Miriam retired and returned to North America, having served 40 and 38 years respectively. In February 1983 four additional pastors were ordained: Naaman Agola, Elifaz Odundo, and Hellon Omolo for the South Nyanza area, and Joshua Okello for the Nairobi congregation (begun in 1975). By this time the Kenya Mennonite Church numbered 50 congregations and 2,500 members.

3. The leprosarium buildings then became available to establish Michire Secondary School.

4. A correlation has been established between the incidence of malaria and of Burkett's Lymphoma; the research is continuing.

## Chapter 9

1. See page 80, "With the Lord." Pastor Yeremia M. Kabury and Deacon Paulo C. Chemere died in 1984.

2. Nyarero Vocational School was established in the facilities of the former Mara Hills School, elementary school for the children of missionaries 1952-66.

## Chapter 10
1. A selection of persons from the major streams of church history: Orthodox, Catholic, and Protestant.
2. Downers Grove, Ill.; InterVarsity Press, 1984.

# IV. BIBLIOGRAPHY, SOURCES OF INFORMATION

## A. ESSAYS, LETTERS

Abura, Musa A.
Birai, Naftali and Elizabeth
Bubalo, Sylvia
Busanya, James M.
Butiku, Ezra
Chirangi, A. M.
Cressman, Elsie
Dhaje, Nikanor
Eshleman, Lester and Lois
Eshleman, Merle
Ferster, Maybell
Frantz, Tom
Gershon, Tumaini
Hurst, Simeon
Igira, Rachel
Jacobs, Donald
Kaema, K. J.
Karamba, Elkana M.
Kasonde, Bukori E.
Kawira, Manaen
Kibira, Emmanuel B.
Kisare, Zedekia M.
Kurtz, Laura
Leatherman, Catharine
Mabeba, Maragesi
Magangira, J. Wera
Magare, Marshall O.
Magare, Miriam O.
Magenda, Eliakim
Mahemba, Daudi W.
Makonyu, Lawrence S.
Marara, Yeremia

Marukwa, Ebanda K.
Mauma, Eliam M.
Mbeba, Joram and Ludia
Mbira, Philemon K.
Muganda, Josiah M.
Muganda, Michael M.
Muganda Samuel
Mummau, Jeanette
Muttani, Sospeter M.
Ndaro, Stephano
Ngoya, Dishon M.
Nyamagundu, Salmon M.
Nyambalya, George
Nyambok, Nashon K.
Nzesi, Velma E.
Obiero, Isaya and Priskilla
Obonyo, Eliakim N.
Okach, Wilson O.
Okidi, Jeremia
Oloko, Samuel N.
Onyiego, Jairo A.
Peters, Gordon
Rhobi, Family of Nathanael
Rufenacht, Verle
Sarya, Hezekia N.
Sattima, Daniel M.
Shenk, J. Clyde
Shenk, Joseph C.
Sigira, Daniel M.
Smoker, George
Tingayi, Mahlon
Tingayi, Nathanael and Damari
Wenger, Rhoda

## B. INTERVIEWS

Agutu, Salome M.
Ayoo, Gershon
Brubaker, Jere
Bumangi District Council
Bunda District Council
  (and a few teachers)
Butiku, Joseph
Dar es Salaam Distr. Council
Dhaje, Bethseba
Dorsch, Victor and Viola
Itinde, Nyerere and Mirembe
Japhet, Adonias
Kaitira, Naftali and Ludia N.
Karuguru, Stanislaus
Kawira, Enoka and Trufena
Kawira, Josiah
Kerario, Daudi
Mabeba, Rebeka
Macha, Anaeli
Maiga, Arphaxad
Maira, Zilipa
Majita District Council
Marwa, Salome
Maxwell, Daniel
Migire, Zephania
Miller, Harold
Mtoka, Daniel I.
Mtoka, Lois M.
Muganda, Raheri
Mugango District Council
Musoma District Council
Musyangi, Paulo
Nathanael, Dina

Ndege, Stackus
Newswanger, Stella
Ngoga, Samuel
Ngeiyamu, Joel
Nyabasi District Council
Nyagwaswa, Matt
Nyambalya, Nashon
Nyambalya, Robert
Nyamhangata, Jonathan
Nyambok, Dorka K.
Nyang'oro, Phinehas
Nyarusanda, Gershon
Ocheche, Magare
Ochuodho, Elifaz
Odhiambo, Narkiso and Peris
Ogwada, Wilson
Okoll, Nyenje
Oole, Daniel O.
Otulo, Simeon and Martha
Philemon, Priskilla
Rogoro District Council
Samson, Rebeka
Serikali, Mwikwabai
Smoker, Dorothy
Stauffer, Grace
Tieng'o, Priska Y.
Togoro, Koreni and Rhoda
Uromi, Ambroz
Wambura, Yakobo
Wandiba, Eliya
Wadugu, Manaen and Kezia
Wenger, Daniel
Yoya, Magdalena


## C. PUBLISHED WORKS, DISSERTATIONS

Amolo, Hellon and Meshack Osiro. "Kenya Mennonite Church" in *Mennonite World Hand-book*. Lombard, Ill.: Mennonite World Conference 1978.

Anchak, George Ronald. *An Experience in the Paradox of Indigenous Church Build-ing:* A History of the Eastern Mennonite Mission in Tanganyika, 1934-61. Unpublished Ph.D. dissertation, Michigan State University, 1975.

Anderson, W. B. *The Church in East Africa, 1840-1974*. Dodoma, Tanzania: Central Tanganyika Press, 1977.

Birai, Naftali M. "Tanzania Mennonite Church" *in Mennonite World Handbook*. Lombard, Ill.: Mennonite World Conference, 1978.

Dyck, Cornelius. *An Introduction to Mennonite History*. Scottdale, Pa.: Herald Press, 1967.

Erb, Paul. *Orie O. Miller, the Story of Man and an Era*. Scottdale, Pa.: Herald Press, 1969.

Eshleman, Merle W. *Africa Answers*. Scottdale, Pa.: Mennonite Publishing House, 1951.

Kisare, Z. Marwa, and Shenk, Joseph C., *Kisare, A Mennonite of Kiseru*. Salunga, Pa.: Eastern Mennonite Board of Missions and Charities, 1984.

Kraybill, Paul N., ed. *Called to Be Sent*. Scottdale, Pa.: Herald Press, 1964.

Kurtz, Laura. *An African Education: The Social Revolution in Tanzania*. Brooklyn, N.Y. 11217: Pageant-Poseidon, 1972.

Lederach, Paul M. *Story Collection*. Scottdale, Pa.: Herald Press, 1978.

Migire, Kembo. *Tribal Land Tenure in the North Mara District of Tanzania*. Unpublished M.A. dissertation, Howard University, 1967.

Muganda, Josiah. *The Impact of the Mennonite Mission on Mara Region, Tanzania, 1934-67*. Unpublished M.A. dissertation, Howard University, 1978.

Orr, J. Edwin, *Evangelical Awakenings in Africa*. Minneapolis, Minn.: Bethany Fellowship, 1975.

Schlabach, Theron F. *Gospel versus Gospel*. Scottdale, Pa. : Herald Press, 1980.

Shenk, David W. *Mennonite Safari*. Scottdale, Pa.: Herald Press, 1974.

Sundkler, Bengt, *Bara Bukoba, Church and Community in Tanzania*. London: C. Hurst & Co., 1980.

Zimmerman, Ada M., and Catharine Leatherman. *Africa Calls*. Scottdale, Pa.: Mennonite Publishing House, 1937.

## D. OTHER MANUSCRIPTS

Dorsch, Victor. "An Accurate Picture of the Tanzania Mennonite Church." Fuller Seminary, School of World Mission, 1978.

Jacobs, Donald R. "Reflections on Fifty Years of Tanzanian Church Life." Mennonite Christian Leadership Foundation, 1984.

Lehman, Cora E. "History of Shirati Hospital Emphasizing Nursing Care," Eastern Mennonite College, 1966.

Longenecker, Daniel M. "East Africa Revival Movement: Its Validity and Influence," Eastern Mennonite College, 1968.

Mauma, Eliam. "Miaka Thelathini ya Askofu E. W. Stauffer katika Tanganyika Mennonite Church," Ofisi Kuu KMT, Musoma, 1964.

Mennonite Theological College. "College Echoes," Ofisi Kuu KMT, Musoma, 1965 na 1969.

Muganda, Josiah. "What the Mennonite Mission Accomplished," Eastern Mennonite College, 1964.

Stauffer, Elam W. "Account of God's Working at Shirati, August 1942," Eastern Mennonite Board of Missions, 1942.

Wenger, Daniel. "The Jita Tribe of Mara Region, Tanzania," Lancaster Mennonite High School, 1983.

## E. RESOURCES IN CHURCH HEADQUARTERS
### 1. Salunga, Pa., Eastern Mennonite Board of Missions:
   a. Files of minutes, reports, correspondence.
   b. Official organ, Missionary Messenger, a monthly, 1924 to present.
   c. African Circle Letters, Nos. 1-117 (1934-52).
   d. History of EMBMC 1894-1980, Grace Wenger:

1.XXVI Relations with Mennonite Board of Missions.

1.XXVII Decision to open work in Africa.

2.I.A. Tanzania (92pp).

e. Files of Board of Bishops, Lancaster Mennonite Conference.

The archives of the Lancaster Mennonite Historical Society, Lancaster, Pa., and Archives of the Mennonite Church, Goshen, Ind., also have files and archival holdings relative to EMBMC and a number of missionaries.

## 2. Musoma, Tanzania, Tanzania Mennonite Church:

a. Files of minutes, reports, and correspondence from Church Conference, Council of Ordained Persons and the following committees: Executive, Finance, Evangelism and Outreach, Marriage and Culture, Education, Bible School, Economic Development, Mennonite Center, Medical, Development for Women, Youth and Sunday School, and Mennonite Economic Development Associates (Tanzania). (These are files of total church 1960-80; after 1980 of the Southern Diocese.)

b. Bimonthly *Messenger of Christ,* 1948-1976.

c. Periodic *Voice of TMC,* November 1962-August 1971.

The National Archives, Dar es Salaam, has a few files relating to Mennonite Mission.

## 3. Shirati Mission, Tanzania, Tanzania Mennonite Church:

Files of North Mara Diocese: Church Conference, Council of Ordained Persons, and some of committees named above as from 1980.

## 4. In each church district: Minutes and correspondence of the district council and of the area councils.

**Mahlon M. Hess** is a retired missionary serving with Eastern Mennonite Board of Missions and Charities on special assignments.

A graduate of Eastern Mennonite College, Harrisonburg, Virginia, with a degree in Biblical studies, Hess has done some graduate study in the Biblical Seminary in New York, New York City.

He was ordained in 1940 as a circuit preacher in the Manor District of Lancaster Mennonite Conference. From 1942-45 he served as editor of EMBMC's official periodical, *Missionary Messenger,* and as a director of the board; he taught Bible and missions at Lancaster Mennonite School.

Hess and his family served as missionaries to Tanzania 1945-65. In turn he was a district pastor, administrator of the Mennonite schools, and director of relief and service ministries of the Christian Council of Tanzania.

From 1965-82 he served in promotion and publicity for the mission board, including a second stint as editor of *Missionary Messenger* 1966-74. He also served as copastor of Masonville Mennonite Church and in 1981 and 1982 edited *Lancaster Conference News.*

In 1944 he married Mabel E. Eshleman. Their five children, Alice, Henry, Carl, Dale and Glen, with their spouses, are serving the Lord in a variety of capacities.